FUN with FLAX

Also by Mick Pendergrast

Te Mahi Kete: Maori Basketry for Beginners (1975, 1986)
Feathers and Fibre: A Survey of Traditional and Contemporary
Maori Craft (1984)
Raranga Whakairo: Maori Plaiting Patterns (1984)
Te Aho Tapu: The Sacred Thread (1987)
'The Fibre Arts' in *Maori Art and Culture*, Starzecka et al. (1997)

FUN with FLAX

50 Projects for Beginners

MICK PENDERGRAST
Photographs by Maureen Lander

RAUPO

A RAUPO BOOK
Published by the Penguin Group
Penguin Group (NZ), 67 Apollo Drive, Rosedale,
North Shore 0632, New Zealand (a division of Pearson New Zealand Ltd)
Penguin Group (USA) Inc., 375 Hudson Street,
New York, New York 10014, USA
Penguin Group (Canada), 90 Eglinton Avenue East, Suite 700, Toronto,
Ontario, M4P 2Y3, Canada (a division of Pearson Penguin Canada Inc.)
Penguin Books Ltd, 80 Strand, London, WC2R 0RL, England
Penguin Ireland, 25 St Stephen's Green,
Dublin 2, Ireland (a division of Penguin Books Ltd)
Penguin Group (Australia), 250 Camberwell Road, Camberwell,
Victoria 3124, Australia (a division of Pearson Australia Group Pty Ltd)
Penguin Books India Pvt Ltd, 11, Community Centre,
Panchsheel Park, New Delhi – 110 017, India
Penguin Books (South Africa) (Pty) Ltd, 24 Sturdee Avenue,
Rosebank, Johannesburg 2196, South Africa

Penguin Books Ltd, Registered Offices: 80 Strand, London, WC2R 0RL, England

Originally published by Reed Publishing (NZ) Ltd, 1987
Reprinted 1987, 1988, 1991, 1992, 1994, 1996, 1998, 2000, 2001, 2003 (twice),
2004, 2005, 2006, 2007

First published by Penguin Group (NZ), 2008
5 7 9 10 8 6

Copyright © text Mick Pendergrast, 1987
Copyright © photography Maureen Lander, 1987

The right of Mick Pendergrast to be identified as the author of this work in terms of
section 96 of the Copyright Act 1994 is hereby asserted.

Cover designed by Nicole Merrie
Text designed by Richard King/Edsetera Books Productions
Printed in China through Bookbuilders, Hong Kong

ISBN: 978 0 14 300993 1

A catalogue record for this book is available
from the National Library of New Zealand.

www.penguin.co.nz

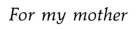

For my mother

ACKNOWLEDGEMENTS

So many people in New Zealand and the Pacific Islands have helped with this book that it is not possible to acknowledge them all individually. First and foremost I must thank those who taught me how to make the individual items. These people are acknowledged at the beginning of each unit of work. My earlier teachers in traditional Māori plaiting crafts must also be mentioned; many craftspeople of Ngāi Tai, Te Whānau-a-Apanui and Ngāti Porou, particularly the late Marara Maihi, Rerekohu Gage and Renata Tihore, would no doubt be surprised to see their instruction and guidance emerging in the present form. Others who have offered much appreciated guidance are Cathie Penetito, Merimeri Penfold, Gabriel Rikihana, Georgina Kirby, Emily Schuster, Val Commins, Poko Morgan, David Simmons, Roger Neich, Mary Best, David Roper, Anne Pendergrast and Roka Paora.

Thanks are also due to Jacob Waghorn, Nathan Sowter, Renee Ngamata and Epiphany Heta, who kindly agreed to pose for photographs.

Most of the toys in the book were learned quite casually, often to fill an odd moment, and originally there was no intention of presenting them in book form. It was much later that I realised that I had gathered a large amount of interesting material over the years, some of it previously unrecorded. When I found that friends and acquaintances were enthusiastic about it, I began to work on my notes and diagrams. Polly Nathan of Āhipara, Itinerant Māori Teacher, finally convinced me that there was a need to have this material published. Thank you, Polly.

CONTENTS

INTRODUCTION

This book is intended to provide a series of projects through which the novice flax-worker can develop a knowledge of basic plaiting skills as an introduction to more advanced Māori flax-crafts. Some items are simple and suitable for very young children; others are more difficult and require some skill. I hope all will be of interest in some way, either for their beauty, use, humour or simply their curiosity value.

For many, the learning and retaining of skills required for traditional Māori plaiting or rāranga is not simple and it is hoped that through the handling and use of flax in the simple articles described, a background of knowledge and skill will evolve to make the step to more difficult items less arduous.

Beginners frequently become discouraged when attempting something difficult, and the making of a kete or Māori kit is not a skill that is picked up in one lesson. An elder once told me that learners should expect to make a hundred kete before the basic principle can be fully mastered.

Teachers in schools or groups often find it difficult to keep enthusiasm alive because they do not have enough activities to interest learners while they are acquiring the skills that will later be used for kete, mats or hats. In school programmes of Māori studies, pupils often learn to make a headband and perhaps a food basket and there it often ends as the teacher is well aware that pupils are not ready to move on to kete making.

I hope that teachers and those trying to teach themselves will find the items described worthwhile and useful for filling the gap between the time when the first flax leaf is split and the stage when fine kete are being produced. From the enthusiasm that some craft experts have shown for many of the toys, I know that some experienced flax plaiters will also find interest and novelty in them.

The directions in the book explain the methods of making fifty items, including toys, novelties and baskets. Some are traditionally Māori, some are developments based on traditional Māori items, but many are from other areas, especially the islands of the South Pacific. They can all be made from New Zealand flax and some could well be made from other materials. Pacific Island children make a large variety of toys from the young leaves of the coconut tree and some of these are included. In Scandinavia, Christmas decorations are made from straw, and the reindeer included is one of these. There is a toy frog from the Indians of the Amazon and a coconut leaf fish from Thailand. All have certain elements in common and all help to develop the skills and knowledge required for the manufacture of Māori kete, mats and hats.

When flax is not available synthetic and manufactured materials such as strips of plastic and ribbon can be used as an alternative for some objects but, although colourful, they are not so attractive as the natural materials, which suit the plaiting crafts so well.

Note: The numerals on the strips in each figure apply to that diagram only. In subsequent diagrams they will apply to new sets of strips.

THE FLAX PLANT

In spite of its name, the so-called New Zealand flax does not belong to the flax family; it is actually a lily. It was called flax by the early traders because of the similarity between its fibre and that of true flax.

There are two species: *Phormium tenax* (figs. i, ii, and iii), the plant that is so much part of the New Zealand swamp scene but will, in fact, grow in a wide range of soils and climates; and the smaller *Phormium cookianum* (previously called *P. colensoi*) (figs. iv and v).

Phormium tenax is known to the Māori as harakeke in most areas although in parts of the Far North it is called kōrari, a name that in other places is reserved for the flower stalk. This is the

FIGURES i, ii and iii
Three varieties of harakeke (*Phormium tenax*) showing different types of leaf.

FIGURES iv and v
Wharariki (*Phormium cookianum*)

plant whose leaves are traditionally used for making baskets, mats, head-bands, food-baskets, and other items, and the fibre of which is used for the manufacture of cloaks and for tāniko finger-weaving.

Phormium cookianum is commonly known as mountain flax, and as wharariki by the Māori. It is usually smaller, with softer, more drooping leaves, which feel thinner when held between the fingers. In some areas it has been used for plaiting mats and baskets, but today it is largely ignored.

Within each species there are numerous varieties — with harder, softer, longer or shorter leaves; with more or less fibre, and varieties variegated or tinged with red, yellow or purple. It is not always easy to determine the species of a particular plant, but one simple way to tell them apart is by examining the seed pods. Those of *P. cookianum* are twisted (fig. vi) and its flowers are often yellow or lime green, while those of *P. tenax* (fig. vii) are not twisted and the flowers are generally red.

Māori people cultivated, and still do, a large number of

FIGURE vi
The twisted seed pods of *Phormium cookianum*

FIGURE vii
The seed pods of harakeke (*Phormium tenax*)

varieties valued for the special properties of their leaves or fibre.

The beginner is advised to spend some time looking at various plants in the area, examining them closely and experimenting with the preparation of leaves from each. Experience is the best teacher here. As a general rule, plants with hard and thick leaves should be avoided as they are very difficult to work with and the results can be unattractive. Soft, flexible leaves that feel thin to the touch are more likely to be suitable.

Harakeke has been the material used for the examples in this book as it is most likely to be available and is usually used for the Māori items which are included. However, wharariki could well be used, and it is worth experimenting with other materials for the sake of experience and variety as well as necessity when harakeke is not available.

HISTORY AND TRADITIONS ASSOCIATED WITH FLAX

When the first settlers arrived in New Zealand they must have been dismayed to find that their treasured coconut palms and bark cloth trees, which provided so many of the necessities of life in tropical Polynesia, were absent and would not grow in the cooler climate.

No doubt they spent some long, hard winters before they discovered substitutes, in particular the plant they named harakeke. Slowly they found ways of utilising it to produce many of the same necessities they had once obtained from the coconut palm, the pandanus and the bark cloth trees.

From its leaves they obtained the fine, soft fibre from which they laboriously manufactured warm and beautiful clothing. It gave them the raw materials for making baskets for carrying food from the gardens, platters to eat from, containers to carry soil and sand for their cultivations and to build up the fortifications around their pā, lines and nets for fishing, mats for sleeping on and to cover floors, bands to hold food in their ovens, lashings for canoes and houses, snares to trap birds, sails for canoes, sandals to protect the feet and, according to legend, even ropes to catch the sun.

From its roots they obtained medicine; from its flowers, nectar; from its pollen, face powder; and from the flower stalks, rafts to cross flooded rivers. The list appears endless, and it is difficult to imagine how they could have survived without harakeke. It is not surprising, therefore, to find a large body of tradition and ritual associated with the plant — its cutting, preparation and manufacturing processes, the articles produced from it, and the initiation of young women into the lore of the Wharepora or House of Weaving. In earlier times it was accepted that the observance of these customs and rituals was a necessary and integral part of successfully acquiring and retaining the skills.

Naturally, the most valued and prestigious articles such as fine cloaks demanded the most stringent practices. In recent times much of the mystery has been transferred to the production of the simpler items such as the kete and whāriki and today these products and their producers are accorded high respect.

Novice flax-workers should know something of the observances and traditions linked with the raw materials and the various processes involved in the craft and so learn a little of the culture from which they sprang. (This subject is discussed in more detail in "The Art of the Whare Pora", by Elsdon Best.)

Sometimes a tradition has an obvious rational basis, and where this is the case, I have given the reason for its observance. In other cases the purpose of the tradition is not so clear.

Cutting flax

Flax should not be cut from the plant in the rain or at night. Rain, frost and cold weather make the leaves hard and difficult to work because of the added moisture.

Burning flax

Flax must not be burned. Scraps of unwanted leaf should be gathered and tied into a bundle and placed under the plant or somewhere else to rot. There is a parallel here with the respect and care accorded to the chips of wood accumulated when a canoe is being built.

Children

Most weavers discourage children from touching, playing with or stepping over the flax being used or the left-over pieces — an admirable tradition.

Eating while working

The majority of plaiters and weavers do not eat while working. The connections between food and tapu are many and complex, but it is also worth remembering that the best work will probably result if the flax-worker's attention is undivided.

Women

Women with their mate wahine (menstrual periods) do not go to the flax plant. Another destroyer of tapu.

Stepping over flax and unfinished work

This is forbidden. It applies especially to women and is probably related to the menstrual cycle. However, it is often seen as a respect for the flax and as such applies to men and children as well.

Perseverance

An article once started must be completed. If it is not, the weaver will not make progress in the art nor retain the skills learned. If students are not keen enough to stick at the work until it is finished, they probably won't be keen enough to practise the skills until they are properly mastered.

Selling your work

Some workers do not favour the selling of traditional craft work. Others make it especially for sale.

A point in favour of selling is that this is the only way in which most people can own an article of Māori craft. The finest work is usually produced by a weaver who is completely involved and dedicated to the work in hand and not concerned with material gain. In my experience, the finest Māori plaited work is not for sale but is freely given to well-loved friends and relations.

Your first completed article

It is usual for the first article in any new craft to be given away (or sometimes buried).

Unsightly as the first effort may be, it is a valued gift to the expert weaver, who sees not its unshapeliness but the effort and concentration that went into it. To receive a first kit from a learner is taken as a compliment by an experienced weaver, and teachers are often given their pupils' first efforts.

There are also traditions about how kete should be given away. One kit-maker from the Whakatane area never gives away a kete unless there is something in it — a bar of chocolate, an apple or some money. Another old lady from the Far North leaves the hairy pieces of fibre on a finished kete if she is to give it away. The person to whom it is given will remove them, creating a mystical bond between the two, the artist and the recipient of the kete.

SELECTION, CUTTING AND PREPARATION OF FLAX

The end product of any craft work depends very largely upon the skill of the worker, but in the case of flax-crafts the initial selection of a suitable variety of flax can have a considerable bearing. For instance, the leaves of some plants are so thick and hard that it is almost impossible to plait them into neat, well-finished articles. The leaves of certain plants may dry out to a very attractive golden colour and some to a clean, clear white, which enhances the completed work. Some plants are more suitable for making a particular article than others. Some flax plants are cultivated for the quality of the fibre they produce, others are valued for their long leaves, especially suitable for mat-making.

The beginner can learn to select only by experience, although an expert flax-worker in the district may be happy to offer advice. Take a strip about 15 mm wide from a leaf and draw it across the back of a knife blade, as shown in fig. xi. If the knife runs freely along, softening the leaf as it goes, the plant is probably suitable, but if the strip is hard and unyielding, it is likely to be too hard to work with. Leaving the leaf in the sun for an hour or so may help to soften it.

Stiff, upright leaves are usually harder to work with than ones that droop at their tips, but this does not always apply. Some leaves contain more moisture than others and will shrink more as they dry; some will dry to a more attractive colour than others. It is worth taking the time to experiment with the properties of different varieties.

Cultivating selected plants in the home garden is a good investment, as regular and careful cutting and cleaning can often improve the texture of the leaf. However, do not be surprised if plants brought in from another area alter their appearance and characteristics in a different soil or climate.

Cutting

When a suitable plant has been selected, the leaves are harvested. The central shoot, called the rito (1 in fig. viii), and the leaves on either side of it (2 in fig. viii) should not normally be cut as doing so weakens the plant considerably and also these leaves tend to shrink more than more mature ones as they dry.

The next leaves (3 in fig. viii) outside the three central ones are used for plaiting. From two to six will generally be taken from

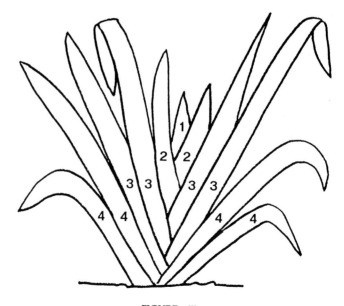

FIGURE viii

each fan of leaves. They are cut with a downward motion with a sharp knife, as near as possible to where they join the fan.

The older tattered leaves (4 in fig. viii) should also be cut to encourage new growth and to make the next cutting easier.

Splitting

To split the leaves into strips for plaiting, press the two halves or sections of a leaf together and, with the thumbnail of the right hand, make slits in the leaf, starting near the midrib and working towards the outer edges of the leaf (fig. ix). The slits are made so that the resulting strips will be an even width for the work in hand.

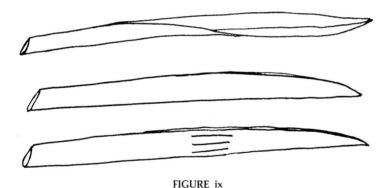

FIGURE ix

Thread the first finger of the right hand through the slits and draw it towards the tip of the leaf, splitting it into long, even strips (fig. x). Now split the leaf back towards the butt end until the point is reached where the leaf becomes hard and unyielding, then cut off the waste butt. The midrib and thin outer edges are also discarded.

Scraping

The strips are individually scraped to soften them and to make them more flexible. This also removes some of the excess moisture and encourages the flax to dry to a better colour without too

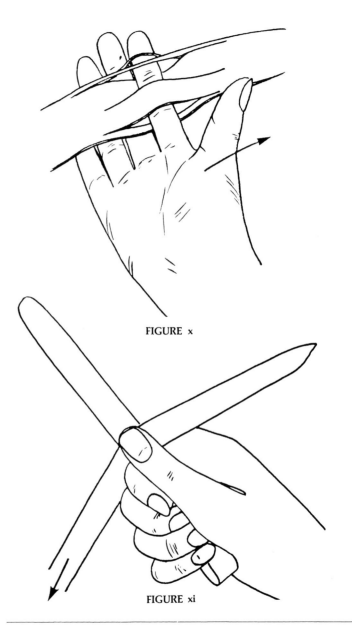

FIGURE x

FIGURE xi

much rolling or shrinkage. The dull underside of the strip is held tightly against the back of the blade of a knife with the thumb, as shown in fig. xi. Pull the strip between the thumb and the back of the blade of the knife with the left hand in the direction indicated by the arrow.

For a long strip it is sometimes easier to start at the middle of the strip and scrape towards the thin pointed end, then reverse the leaf and scrape towards the butt end.

Now turn the strip over and treat the shiny, upper surface in the same way. The strip should now feel much softer. This is not an easy process to master and requires practice.

The preparation and selection of the flax takes practice and experience. No hard and fast rules can be laid down because the leaves of individual flax plants will shrink and harden in different ways and the process is affected by the weather.

Leaves cut when they have had hot sunshine on them for many hours will have less moisture in them, will be thinner and feel softer to work with. They will not shrink as much as harder, more brittle flax, especially if it has had rain on it, it grows in a very wet position or has been subjected to cold weather.

Flax leaves should be treated differently according to the weather. On a hot sunny day, a few hours in a shady place and then an hour or so in the sun will soften them and drive out excess moisture. In the winter, leaves may be more workable after being stored in a shed for up to a week and then warmed in front of a fire or heater, both before and after scraping.

A close watch must be kept to see that the flax does not become too dry and brittle as it will then begin to roll up. If it has just begun to roll, the scraping process will usually flatten it, but if left any longer, there is not much that can be done with it.

If flax is to be kept for long periods in the summer it can be wrapped tightly in a damp bag and stored in a cool place or stood in a large container of water until needed.

Preparation of boiled flax

Note: All the items described in this book can be made from raw flax. Preparation of boiled flax is included for those who wish to experiment with it.

One of the attributes of flax leaves is the way in which they shrink as they dry. Sometimes this is desirable as in a kit to be used for kūmara or shell fish. The open mesh allows soil adhering to the kūmara to separate from the tubers, leaving them clean for storing. In the case of shell fish, sand or mud can be washed away without taking them from the kit.

In most of the objects described here a closer weave is desirable and as much shrinkage as possible should take place before the actual plaiting begins. Before making fine mats and kits, both flax and kiekie are often immersed in boiling water, a process that shrinks the strips and whitens them. In the Pacific Islands the same result is obtained by cooking pandanus leaves and then bleaching them in the sun. In some parts the pandanus leaves are still cooked in an earth oven. Māori flax-workers probably used a similar method before the arrival of metal containers, which made the boiling of water a simple matter.

Before boiling, the unscraped strips of flax are tied into small bundles at the tips. The water must be boiling strongly so that it will not go off the boil when the cold strips are immersed in it. The bundles are then held in boiling water for up to five minutes. Usually one end is held in the water and then the bundle reversed so the other end can be treated in the same way. The strips of flax turn a bright green and the water runs off them in drops when they are done. The cooked bundles are placed in cold water for some time before being hung in the shade, preferably in a draughty position, until all the excess water has drained off them and they are partly dry. If they are allowed to become too dry, the process of scraping them will be difficult or perhaps impossible.

The slightly damp strips are now scraped across the back of the blade of a knife, or traditionally a mussel shell, as shown in fig. xi.

Boiled flax can be stored when properly dry. Before using for plaiting, it is moistened by wrapping in a damp towel for a few hours and then scraped again.

THE PROJECTS

UNIT 1
Tipare (a headband)

The braid commonly used by concert parties to make headbands is called mekameka by Ngāti Porou. The headbands themselves are known as tīpare in the North Island and as kōpare in the South.

The same braid is also used in many Pacific Islands and in Europe, where it is known as the Tyrolean plait. I learned it from the children of Ngāi Tai at Tōrere in 1954.

Take two strips of flax leaf about 3 cm wide and as long as possible. Prepare them as described on p. 10. Split each of the strips down the middle, leaving about 6 cm unsplit at the butt end of each. A fold across the leaf near the butt helps to prevent it from splitting.

Place the strips in position as shown in fig. 1.2.

Strip 1 in fig. 1.2 is folded along the dotted line, over the two strips to the right of it and under the third strip, as indicated by the arrow, to lie in the position shown in fig. 1.3.

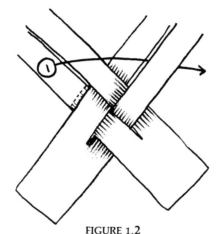

FIGURE 1.2

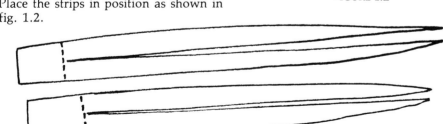

FIGURE 1.1

Strip 1 in fig. 1.3 is folded along the dotted line, over the strip to the left of it and under the next one, as indicated by the arrow, to lie in the position shown in fig. 1.4. There are now two strips pointing in each direction.

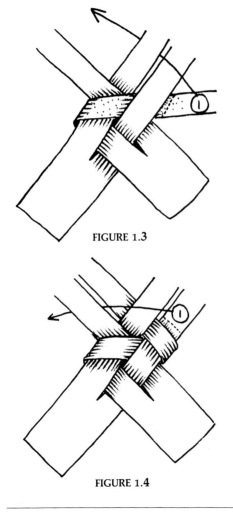

FIGURE 1.3

FIGURE 1.4

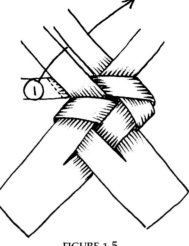

FIGURE 1.5

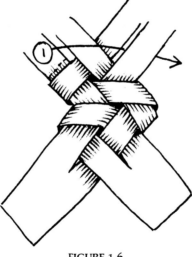

FIGURE 1.6

Strip 1 in fig. 1.4 is folded along the dotted line, over the two strips to the left of it and under the third strip, as indicated by the arrow, to lie in the position shown in fig. 1.5.

Strip 1 in fig. 1.5 is folded along the dotted line, over the first strip and under the second, as indicated by the arrow, to lie in the position shown in fig. 1.6.

The next movement, shown in fig. 1.6, is the same as that already worked in fig. 1.2. Strip 1 in fig. 1.6 (or fig. 1.2) is folded along the dotted line, over the first two strips to the right of it and under the third strip, as indicated by the arrow, to lie in the position shown in fig. 1.3.

Work the movements shown in figs. 1.3, 1.4 and 1.5 and repeat until the headband is long enough. When a strip gets too short to use, wait until you make a movement in which the short strip crosses the braid at right angles (strip 1 in fig. 1.7).

FIGURE 1.7

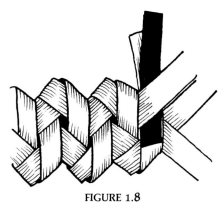

FIGURE 1.8

Place a new strip of leaf into the braid on top of the short strip 1, as shown in fig. 1.8. The new strip is shown in black.

Continue to braid until the band is long enough to reach around the head with 3 to 6 cm overlapping. The overlapping pieces are either tied or sewn together with thin strips of flax. The spare ends are trimmed off.

Wearing the headband

Headbands are normally worn low on the brow in a horizontal line, not stuck on the back of the head. In some areas it is not correct to wear feathers in the band, a couple of strips of flax being used as trim instead. Perhaps this is because the feathers worn as ornaments by the Māori were rare and highly valued and therefore not to be worn in such a temporary and makeshift article as a headband.

An alternative beginning

Lay two strips of prepared flax 1.5 cm wide in the positions shown in fig. 1.9.

Fold strip 1 in fig. 1.9 along the dotted line, in the direction indicated by the arrow, to lie in the position shown in fig. 1.10.

Fold strip 1 in fig. 1.10 *back* along the dotted line, in the direction indicated by the arrow, to lie in the position shown in fig. 1.11.

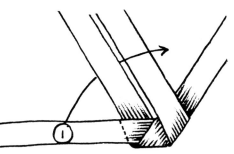

FIGURE 1.10

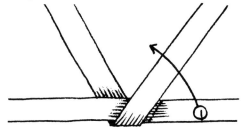

FIGURE 1.9

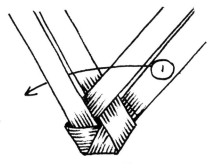

FIGURE 1.11

Fold strip 1 in fig. 1.11 along the dotted line, in the direction indicated by the arrow, to lie in the position shown in fig. 1.12. Continue to follow the directions indicated in figs. 1.11, 1.12, 1.13 and 1.14. The movements are exactly the same as those already practised in the first series of figures.

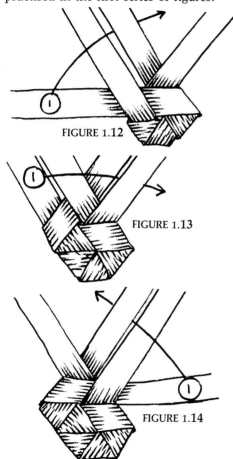

FIGURE 1.12

FIGURE 1.13

FIGURE 1.14

U N I T   2
Another headband

This variation on the mekameka was shown to me by Kei Whare at Tautoro, near Kaikohe, about 1960. It was well known in the area at the time.

Prepare two strips of flax about 3 cm wide and as long as possible.

Fold strip 1 in fig. 2.1 along the dotted line and across all three of the other strips, as indicated by the arrow, to lie in the position shown in fig. 2.2.

Fold strip 1 in fig. 2.2 *back* along the dotted line, under the strip to the left of it, and over the next one, as indicated by the arrow, to lie in the position shown in fig. 2.3.

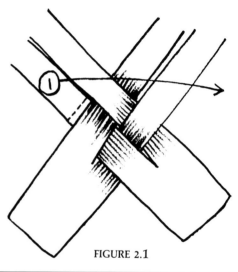

FIGURE 2.1

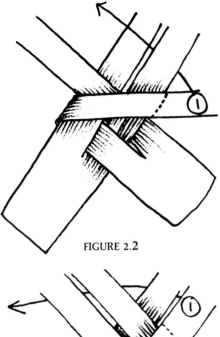

FIGURE 2.2

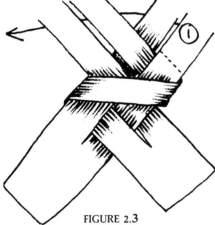

FIGURE 2.3

Fold strip 1 in fig. 2.3 *back* along the dotted line and under all the other strips, as indicated by the arrow, to lie in the position shown in fig. 2.4.

Fold strip 1 in fig. 2.4 along the dotted line, over the strip to the right of it and under the next one, as indicated by the arrow, to lie in the position shown in fig. 2.5.

The movement shown in fig. 2.5 is the same as that already shown in fig. 2.1. Strip 1 is folded along the dotted line and over all the other strips.

Continue to work the figures until the headband is long enough, and then finish off as explained in unit 1.

Joins are made when a strip is crossing diagonally, and the old strip is carried with the new for a complete movement.

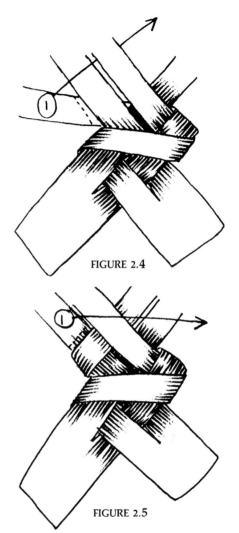

FIGURE 2.4

FIGURE 2.5

UNIT 3
Headband using six strips

This is a braid very similar to the mekameka but using six strips instead of four.

Prepare three strips of flax, each about 1 cm wide and as long as possible. Lay two strips out in the positions shown in fig. 3.1.

Fold strip 1 in fig. 3.1 along the dotted line, in the direction indicated by the arrow, to lie in the position shown in fig. 3.2.

Fold strip 1 in fig. 3.2 *back* along the dotted line, in the direction indicated by the arrow, to lie in the position shown in fig. 3.3.

Insert the third strip in the position shown in fig. 3.4.

Fold strip 1 in fig. 3.4 along the dotted line, in the direction indicated by the arrow. Fold strip 2 in fig. 3.4 *back* along the dotted line, in the direction indicated by the arrow. The work should now look like fig. 3.5

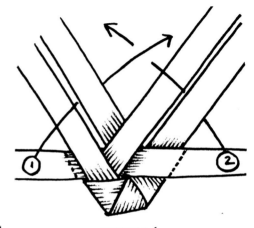

FIGURE 3.4

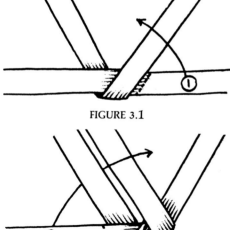

FIGURE 3.1

FIGURE 3.2

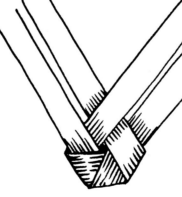

FIGURE 3.3

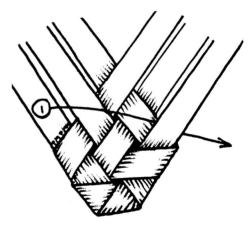

FIGURE 3.5

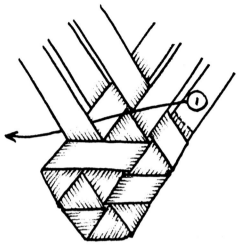

FIGURE 3.7

Fold strip 1 in fig. 3.5 along the dotted line, in the direction indicated by the arrow, to lie in the position shown in fig. 3.6. It passes over four strips and under one.

Fold strip 1 in fig. 3.6 along the dotted line and in the direction indicated by the arrow to lie in the position shown in fig. 3.7. It passes over one, under one, over one.

Fold strip 1 in fig. 3.7 along the dotted line and in the direction indicated by the arrow to lie in the position shown in fig. 3.8. It passes over four strips and under one.

Fold strip 1 in fig. 3.8 along the dotted line and in the direction indicated by the arrow. It moves over one, under one, over one. The working edge should now look the same as that illustrated in fig. 3.5.

Continue to work figs. 3.5, 3.6, 3.7 and 3.8 until the band is long enough. Joins are made and the work finished as described in unit 1.

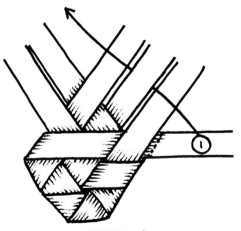

FIGURE 3.6

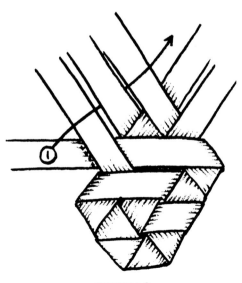

FIGURE 3.8

U N I T   4
Table mat using the mekameka braid

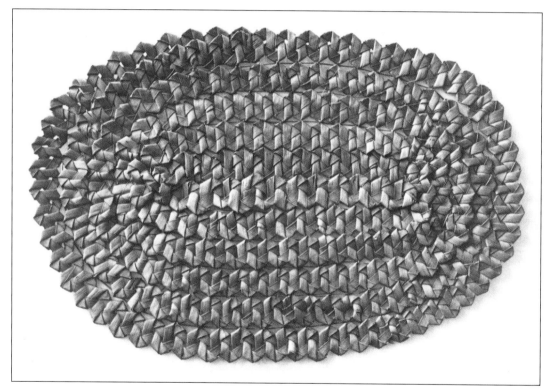

To make a table mat using the mekameka braid, prepare a very long braid following the directions for the tīpare (unit 1). This is then sewn into a spiral using a large needle and a narrow strip of flax.

For an oval mat, lay out about 20 cm of braid and then work the next section around so that it doubles back along the side of the first section. The rows may be slightly overlapped, which is the usual method, or if the braid is even, joined together at the points as shown in fig. 4.1.

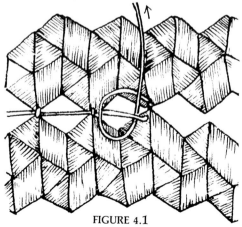

FIGURE 4.1

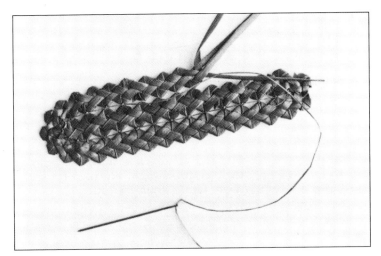

FIGURE 4.2

FIGURE 4.3

Fig. 4.2 shows the first round.

Continue to sew the strip into a spiral until the mat is the desired size. Fig. 4.3 shows the stitching on the back of the mat.

Because of the stiffness of the flax, it is difficult to bring the braid around the corners neatly, especially in the first few rounds when the corners are sharp. To overcome this difficulty a rectangular mat may be made, with the corners worked into the strip. Figs. 4.4, 4.5, 4.6 and 4.7 demonstrate the method of working the corner. The actual braid is not difficult, but a little practice is required to get the corners in the positions required. Work one corner at a time and then sew it into place in the main body of the mat before proceeding to the next corner.

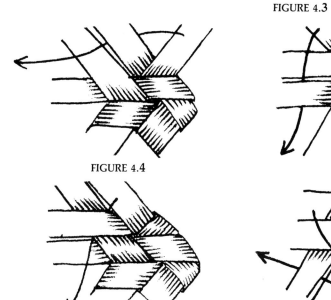

FIGURE 4.4

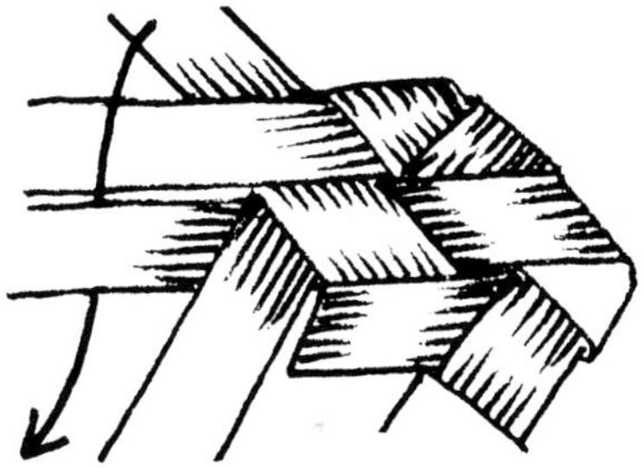

FIGURE 4.6

FIGURE 4.5

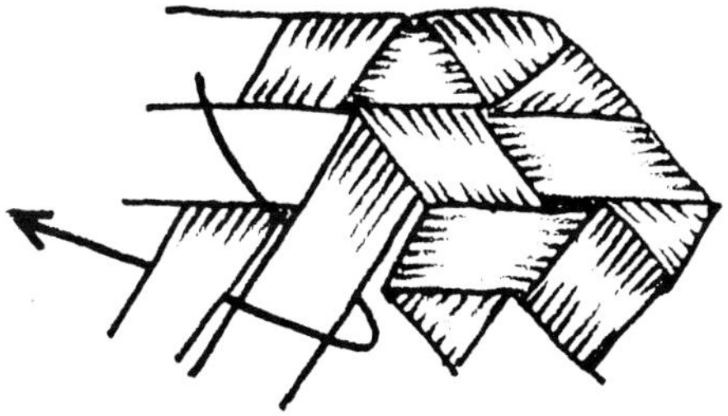

FIGURE 4.7

23

UNIT 5
Hats and kits using the mekameka braid

Kits and hats are sometimes made using the mekameka braid practised for the tīpare (unit 1) and the technique used for the table mat (unit 4).

The late Papakahawai Herewini of Ngāi Tai was shown how to make kits and hats using the mekameka braid at the turn of the century before she began to make kete. At that time it was common practice to give very young girls this type of work as a form of apprenticeship. In Papakahawai's case, the material used was the inner bark of the houhi (lacebark).

For the kit, begin by making a long mekameka braid as was done for the tīpare (unit 1) and lay out as much of it as is required for the base of the kit. Then fold the strip sharply back and alongside itself as was done for the table mat (unit 4). Again, the first corner is the most difficult. After one or two rounds, which will form the bottom of the kit, begin to work up the sides in the same way, sewing the strips together as the work progresses until the kit is tall enough.

Handles can be made separately using the three-ply braid (unit 27) and sewn into the positions required, or attached as for the windmill knot kit (unit 13).

The hat is made in a similar way. Again, make a long braid of mekameka, then sew it into a spiral. The beginning of the spiral becomes the centre of the crown of the hat. The shaping of the crown and the brim is done as the work proceeds, simply by sewing the mekameka strip into the desired position a small section at a time. The most difficult part is the beginning, where the plait has to be sharply twisted around, and this is especially difficult when flax is used.

UNIT 6
Windmill

The Māori windmill toy, known in New Zealand as titi pārera, is well known in many other parts of the Pacific, where it is commonly made from coconut leaflets. In New Zealand it is made from either flax or raupo, and the following charm was recorded by W.J. Phillipps (1955). It was addressed to the Wind God as the children spun the toy by facing it into the wind on a short length of fern stalk.

Hōmai rā he hau mō taku tītiti pārerera
Give me some wind for my tītiti pārerera
Note: tītiti pārerera is an alternative form of the name

Te Rangihiroa (1927) describes such a toy from Aitutaki in the Cook Islands as being made from coconut leaflets and called porotaka.

The same knot is used as a bait rest in the Māori fish trap called tōrehe, but here the windmill is made from supplejack or pirita (*Rhipogonum scandens*) (Te Rangihiroa: 1926).

Take two strips of flax leaf about 2 cm wide and 40 to 50 cm long.

Twist one of the strips around the first two fingers of the left hand as shown in fig. 6.1. Remove from the fingers. You now have a loop as shown in fig. 6.2.

Place the second strip through the loop as shown in fig. 6.3.

Strip 1 in fig. 6.3 is taken *behind* the work, as indicated by the arrow, and brought to the position shown in fig. 6.4.

The same strip is then carried over one strip and through the original loop, as indicated by the arrow in fig. 6.4, to the position shown in fig. 6.5.

The knot is tightened by pulling on the ends of all strips as indicated by the arrows. The knot is now complete and should look like fig. 6.6.

Trim the ends of the windmill so that they are of equal length. A hole is pierced through the centre so that a small stick can be put through. The windmill spins on the stick when held into the wind.

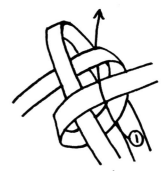

FIGURE 6.4

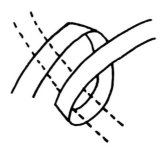

FIGURE 6.2

FIGURE 6.5

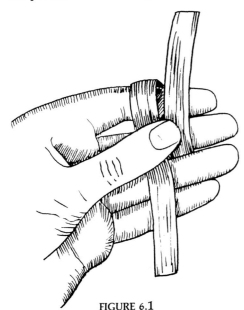

FIGURE 6.1

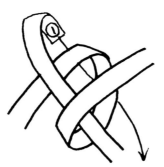

FIGURE 6.3

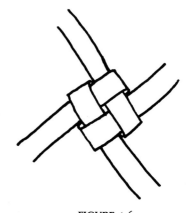

FIGURE 6.6

UNIT 7
Angel fish

The angel fish was made by boys from many islands at Maravovo School on Guadalcanal in the Solomons in 1970. It is a simple continuation of the windmill (unit 6) and can be suspended from a fine thread as part of a mobile.

Prepare two strips of flax about 2 cm wide and 40 to 50 cm long. First tie the windmill knot described in unit 6. Now turn the knot over so that it lies in the position shown in fig. 7.1.

Fold strip 1 in fig. 7.1 in the direction indicated by the arrow to lie in the position shown in fig. 7.2.

FIGURE 7.2

FIGURE 7.1

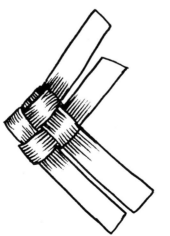

FIGURE 7.3

Fold strip 2 in fig. 7.2 forward on itself and under strip 3, as indicated by the arrow. To do this, strip 1 will need to be moved aside. Tighten all strips. The work should now look like fig. 7.3.

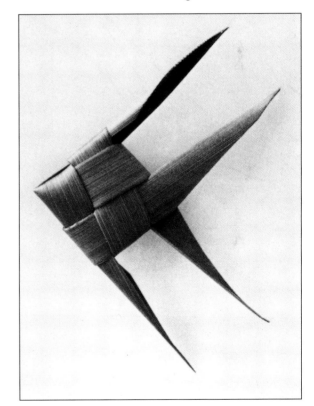

Trim the fins and tail with a pair of scissors to the shapes shown in fig. 7.4. A fine strip of leaf or other thread is tied to the upper fin to suspend the completed toy.

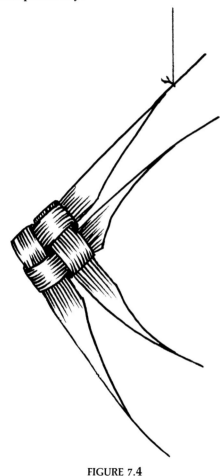

FIGURE 7.4

U N I T   8
Person

A toy person can be made from the angel fish (unit 7). Make the angel fish but leave the fins and tail longer to become the arms and legs. Attach a head at the top with a narrow strip of flax. The head can be the square ball (unit 33), a nut, a seed, or simply a suitable leaf.

A similar person can also be made after completing fig. 18.6 of the fish (unit 18).

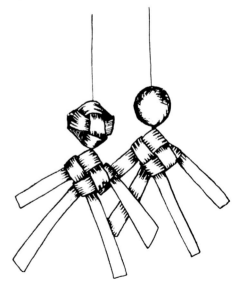

U N I T 9
Wasp nest

This is a child's toy in which the windmill (unit 6) is further developed. It is also a practice item for the Fijian necklace (unit 10), which uses the same technique. The same braid was used by the Māori to make a rope (Phillipps, 1955).

Prepare two strips of flax about 1 cm wide and as long as possible. First tie a windmill (unit 6), as already described. Turn the work over as shown in fig. 9.1.

Fold strip 1 in fig. 9.1 along the dotted line, in the direction indicated by the arrow, to lie in the position shown in fig. 9.2.

Fold strip 1 in fig. 9.2 along the dotted line, in the direction indicated by the arrow, to lie in the position shown in fig. 9.3.

Fold strip 1 in fig. 9.3 along the dotted line, in the direction indicated by the arrow, to lie in the position shown in fig. 9.4.

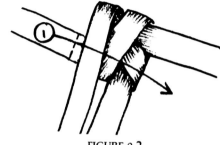

FIGURE 9.2

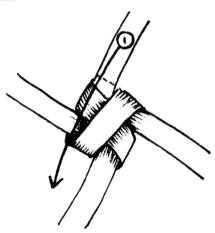

FIGURE 9.1

FIGURE 9.3

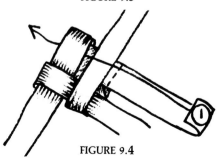

FIGURE 9.4

Strip 1 in fig. 9.4 is folded and moved as indicated by the arrow. It passes over one and under one. The work should now look like fig. 9.5.

Fold strip 1 in fig. 9.5 along the dotted line, in the direction indicated by the arrow, to lie in the position shown in fig. 9.6.

Strip 1 in fig. 9.6 is folded along the dotted line, in the direction indicated by the arrow, to lie in the position shown in fig. 9.7.

Strip 1 in fig. 9.7 is folded along the dotted line, in the direction indicated by the arrow, to lie in the position shown in fig. 9.8.

Strip 1 in fig. 9.8 is folded along the dotted line and in the direction indicated by the arrow. It passes over one strip and under strip 2. The work is locked again and should look like fig. 9.9.

Repeat the sequence following the movements suggested by the arrows and numerals in fig. 9.9. The work is locked by passing under the last strip as in fig. 9.8. Repeat as often as desired. The sequence of each four movements is in the opposite direction to the previous sequence. Cut off the waste and the toy is complete.

A number of wasp nests can be made into a satisfactory mobile. They can also be used to make a necklace, interspacing the wasp nests with beads, seeds or pieces of wood.

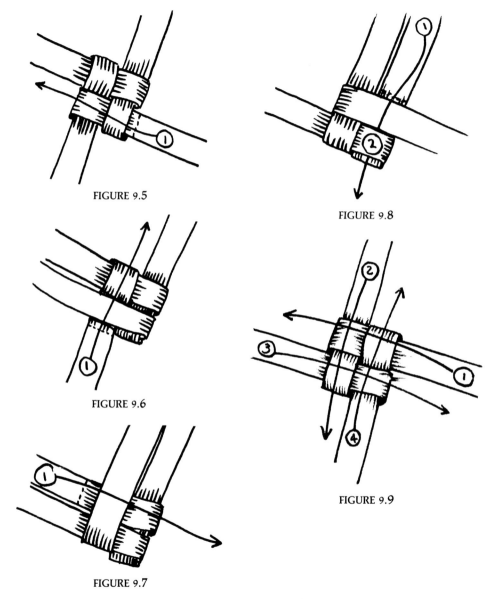

FIGURE 9.5

FIGURE 9.8

FIGURE 9.6

FIGURE 9.9

FIGURE 9.7

UNIT 10
Fijian necklace

This attractive braid is used to suspend the highly valued tabua or whale's tooth in the Fiji Islands. I learnt it on Kabara Island in 1967 using strips of dried pandanus, but the Fijians also use cord made of coconut coir. A rope is made in the same way to attach white cowrie shells to the yaqona or kava bowl in front of the chief.

Prepare a number of strips of flax about 0.5 cm wide and as long as possible. Select two of the strips and tie them together at the centre with a windmill knot (unit 6). Now proceed to braid the four ends into a wasp nest (unit 9).

At intervals relief and variety are provided by a gap in which there is no braid. This can be done at any stage. After the work has been locked as in the wasp nest, follow fig. 10.1 for the arrangement of the strips. Once they are in position, revert again to the movements for the wasp nest.

Joins are made by inserting a new strip on the old strip that is becoming too short and braiding them together for a single movement, then dropping the old strip and carrying on with the new one alone. In the pandanus cord the waste ends are split and left as ornaments, but flax is too stiff to do this satisfactorily and they are better cut off.

FIGURE 10.1

UNIT 11
Spectacles

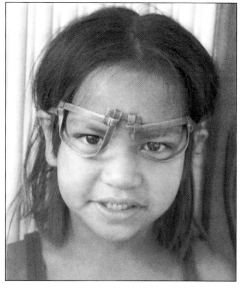

Making glasses out of coconut leaflet affords island children much amusement. The two types shown, I saw at Maravovo on Guadalcanal in the Solomon Islands in 1970. They can both be made from flax strips and both use the windmill knot (unit 6).

Prepare two strips of flax about 1 cm wide. The strips are tied together with windmill knots in the positions required to hold the frames of the spectacles to the desired shape. Fig. 11.1 is the simpler of the two. For fig. 11.2 use three strips of leaf.

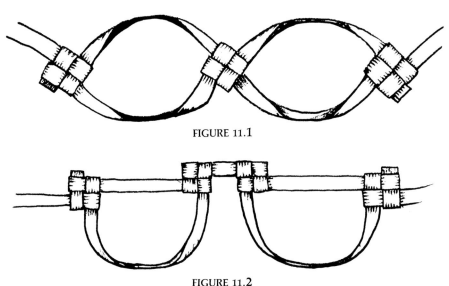

FIGURE 11.1

FIGURE 11.2

UNIT 12
Table mat using the windmill knot

In recent times the windmill knot has been adapted and extended to make a number of flax items. I first saw this table mat in Ōpotiki in 1969, made by members of the Ūhengaparāoa Māori Art Co-operative Society, an interested group who attempted, and for some time succeeded, to produce traditional Māori crafts commercially. As well as table mats, teapot stands and long, narrow runners for coffee tables were also made.

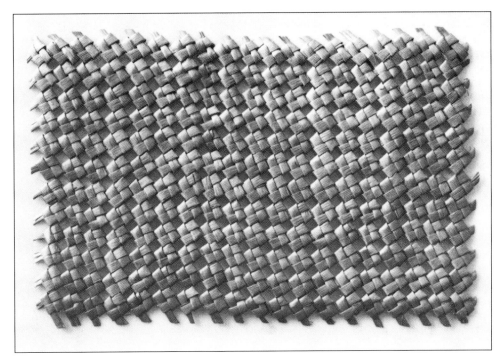

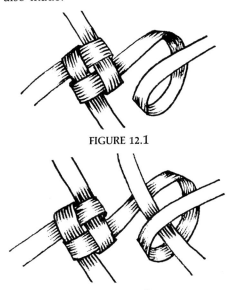

FIGURE 12.1

FIGURE 12.2

Prepare 20 or 30 strips of flax about 1 cm wide and as long as possible. Tie the first knot following the instructions given for the windmill (unit 6).

Loop the strip projecting to the right around the first two fingers of the left hand as in fig. 12.1.

Place a new strip through the loop as in fig. 12.2. This is the same as has already been done for the first knot. Continue to complete the knot as described for the windmill. If the new knot is not touching the first, it must be manipulated until it is. This takes a little practice.

Using the same technique, the third knot is made by looping the strip to the right around the first two fingers of the left hand, and adding a new strip to complete the knot. Continue to tie more knots to the right until the mat is the width you require.

A second row of knots is now added above the completed row. Take a new strip (1 in fig. 12.3) and loop it around the first two fingers of the left hand. Strip 2 in fig. 12.3 is introduced into the knot to complete it. The tying is done in the way already practised. Make sure that the knot is close to the first row of knots.

Strip 1 in fig. 12.4 is now looped around the first two fingers of the left hand and strip 2 (protruding from the first row) introduced into it to tie the knot. Continue along the row in the same way.

The third and succeeding rows are made in exactly the same way, using a new strip for each new row, and introducing a strip from the previous row to tie each knot. Continue to add more rows until the mat is the size you wish.

It is a good idea to add each strip for a new row the opposite way round to the previous one; that is, if one row starts with the butt end of the strip, the next row should begin with the narrow end of the strip. This ensures that the mat is not thinner at one end.

To join

When one strip of leaf becomes too short, a new strip is added by placing the new strip on the top of the old one and tying the next knot with the doubled strip. Trim off any waste.

To finish

When the mat is the size desired, the waste strips protruding around the edges are simply cut off with a pair of scissors, or they can be tucked back under the mat and threaded through the backs of one or two knots. A table mat does not need to be particularly strong and the cut-off ends are usually satisfactory.

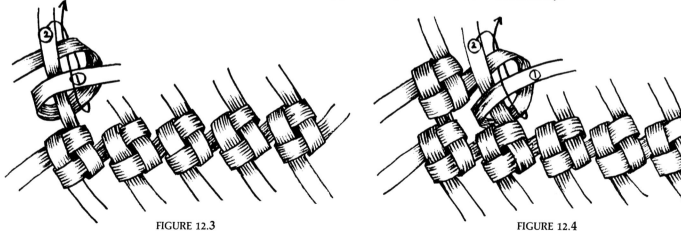

FIGURE 12.3   FIGURE 12.4

UNIT 13
Kit using the windmill knot

I was shown how to make this kit by Nora Hurihanganui of Ngāi Tahu, but it is made in many parts of New Zealand and similar ones are made in some of the Polynesian islands.

Prepare a number of strips about 1 cm wide and as long as possible. Using the same method as has been practised for the table mat (unit 12), tie a row of windmill knots (unit 6) as long as the kit is to be. Now turn the work over so that it lies as in fig. 13.1.

Fold strips 2, 3, 4 and 5 in fig. 13.1 along the dotted lines, in the directions indicated by the arrows, to lie in the positions shown in fig. 13.2. Now fold strip 1 in fig. 13.1 along the dotted line, in the direction indicated by the arrow, to lie in the position shown in fig. 13.2.

Make a loop in strip 1 as shown in fig. 13.3.

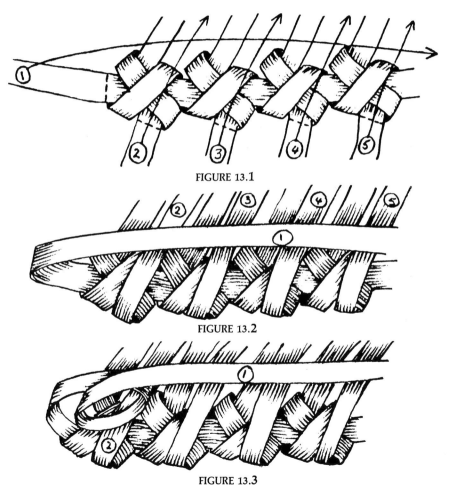

FIGURE 13.1

FIGURE 13.2

FIGURE 13.3

Introduce strip 2 into strip 1 as shown in fig. 13.4.

Complete the windmill knot with strips 1 and 2. Now make the second loop in strip 1, introduce strip 3 into it and make another windmill knot. Treat strip 4 in the same way and continue to tie knots until the row is complete. Then thread the end of the working strip 1 back into and around the first knot that was tied, so completing the circle.

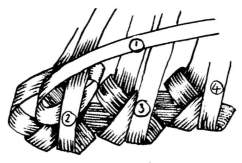

FIGURE 13.4

The bottom of the kit is now formed. A second circle of windmill knots is tied above the first row. Continue to add additional rows until the kit is high enough.

Cut off all the strips at the top of the kit, leaving about 6 cm to tuck back in behind one or two knots.

For the handle, prepare a length of the round four-ply braid (unit 29) or three-ply braid (unit 27) about two metres long. This braid is threaded through the sides of the basket, across the bottom and up the other side, and secured in place with thin strips of flax (fig. 13.5).

FIGURE 13.5

UNIT 14
Frog

This is a toy made by the Bakairi Indians of the Upper Xingu area of Central Brazil (Adams 1963). I have worked out the movements from a single illustration and so, although the final toy looks the same as the traditional one, I cannot be sure that the method of making it is.

Prepare four strips of flax about 2 cm wide and 60 cm long. The first movements are the same as those used for the windmill (unit 6), but instead of using two single strips, each working strip is made up of two strips lying on top of each other. These pairs of strips are treated as single strips in figs. 14.1 to 14.5.

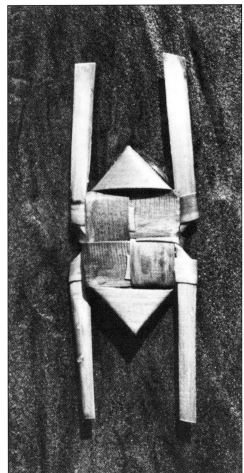

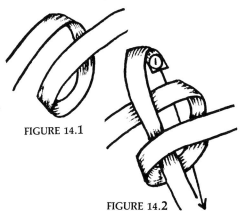

FIGURE 14.1

FIGURE 14.2

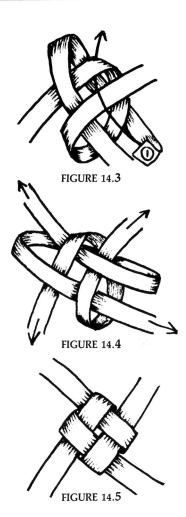

FIGURE 14.3

FIGURE 14.4

FIGURE 14.5

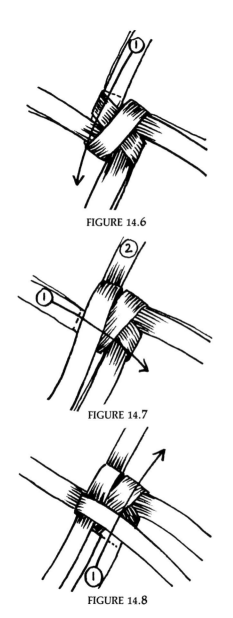

FIGURE 14.6

FIGURE 14.7

FIGURE 14.8

Follow figs. 14.1 to 14.4, which are the same as those already used for the windmill but with doubled strips. The work should look like fig. 14.5 when tightened. Turn the work over as in fig. 14.6.

From now on the strips are used singly. Fold the top strip of pair 1 in fig. 14.6 along the dotted line and fold it back, as indicated by the arrow, to lie in the position shown in fig. 14.7. The lower strip of the pair remains in its original position (strip 2 in fig. 14.7).

The top strip of pair 1 in fig. 14.7 is folded along the dotted line and back on itself, in the direction indicated by the arrow, to lie in the position shown in fig. 14.8.

The top strip 1 in fig. 14.8 is folded along the dotted line and back on itself to lie in the position shown in fig. 14.9.

The single strip 1 in fig. 14.9 is folded along the dotted line and back on itself, as indicated by the arrow. It is passed beneath strip 2. The work should now look like fig. 14.10.

Fold strip 1 in fig. 10 diagonally along the dotted line, in the direction indicated by the arrow, to lie in the position shown in fig. 14.11.

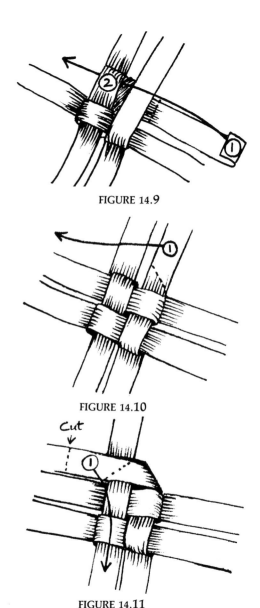

FIGURE 14.9

FIGURE 14.10

FIGURE 14.11

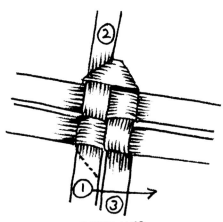

FIGURE 14.12

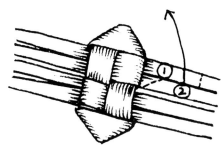

FIGURE 14.13

The same strip 1 in fig. 14.11 is folded again along the second dotted line. This time it is folded *behind* itself and in the direction indicated by the arrow. The strip is then tucked back into the body of the work, but before this can be done it is cut off to a suitable length. The work should now look like fig. 14.12.

Strip 2 in fig. 14.12 is no longer required and is cut off. The head of the frog is now complete. The tail end is made in the same way. Fold strip 1 along the dotted line and move in the direction indicated by the arrow. Now fold it a second time, this time behind itself. After cutting off the excess length, tuck it back into the work. Strip 3 is now cut off. The four remaining strips are each split down the centre so that there are now eight strips as in fig. 14.13.

Fold strip 2 in fig. 14.13 diagonally along the dotted line, in the direction indicated by the arrow, to lie in the position shown in fig. 14.14. Strip 1 is cut off at a suitable length and folded back into the work as indicated by the arrow. This holds strip 2, which is one of the legs, in position. The other legs are treated in the same way and then cut off to a suitable length. The frog is now complete.

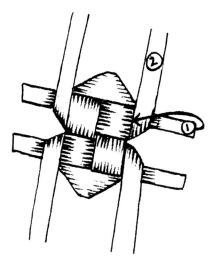

FIGURE 14.14

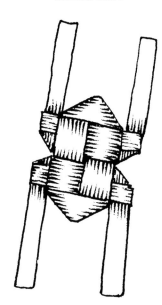

FIGURE 14.15

UNIT 15
First star

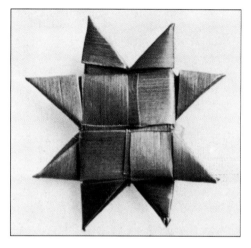

This star uses the first movements of the third star (unit 17) and is included here as a simpler form for practice.

The first movements are made following the movements for figs. 14.1 to 14.10 for the frog (unit 14). Fig. 15.1 shows the work at the end of fig. 14.10 for the frog. Continue from here.

Fold strip 1 in fig. 15.2 diagonally, along the dotted line and in the direction indicated by the arrow to lie in the position shown in fig. 15.3.

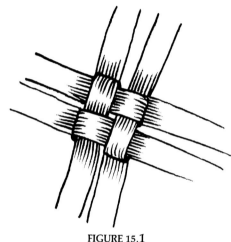

FIGURE 15.1

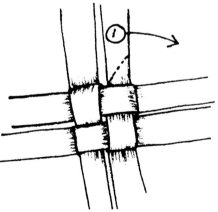

FIGURE 15.2

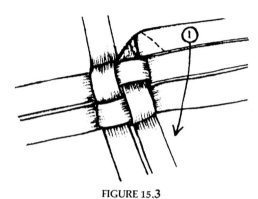

FIGURE 15.3

The same strip 1 in fig. 15.3 is again folded diagonally along the dotted line, in the direction indicated by the arrow, to lie in the position shown in fig. 15.4.

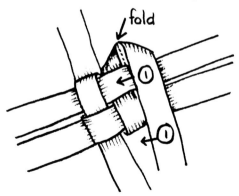

FIGURE 15.4

A third fold is made in the same strip 1 in fig. 15.4 at the dotted line marked with the arrow. The whole strip is now folded over onto itself, as indicated by the arrows, to lie in the position shown in fig. 15.5.

The end of the same strip 1 in fig. 15.5 is threaded under the strip labelled 2. It is pulled through towards the worker to lie in the position shown in fig. 15.6.

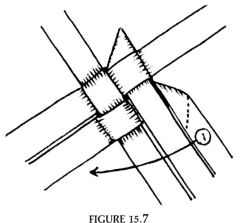

FIGURE 15.7

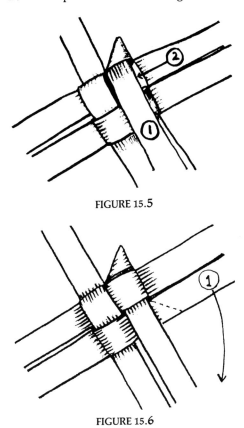

FIGURE 15.5

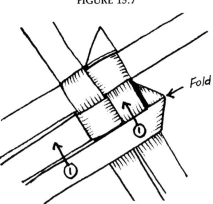

FIGURE 15.8

FIGURE 15.6

Strip 1 in fig. 15.6 is folded under diagonally, along the dotted line and in the direction indicated by the arrow, to lie in the position shown in fig. 15.7.

The same strip 1 in fig. 15.7 is again folded along the dotted line and in the direction indicated by the arrow to lie in the position shown in fig. 15.8.

The same strip 1 in fig. 15.8 is again folded at the point marked, and onto itself, as indicated by the arrows, to lie in the position shown in fig. 15.9.

The same strip 1 in fig. 15.9 is threaded through the loop that lies beneath the position marked with *. The actual loop through which it is threaded is hidden in the diagram by strip 2. The work will now look like fig. 15.10.

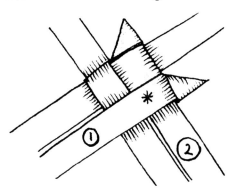

FIGURE 15.9

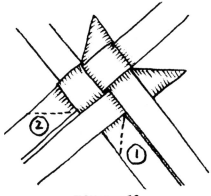

FIGURE 15.10

In the same way, fold strip 1 in fig. 15.10 diagonally along the dotted line, then diagonally again, then onto itself and thread it through the loop beneath. These are the same movements that have already been completed twice.

Strip 2 in fig. 15.10 is treated in the same way. The work will now look like fig. 15.11.

Turn the work over and treat the four strips on the other side in the same manner. Begin as in fig. 15.12.

The work should now look like fig. 15.13.

Cut away the ends of all strips and the first star is complete. Thread it on a strip of flax if it is to be worn as a pendant.

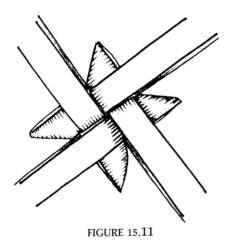

FIGURE 15.11

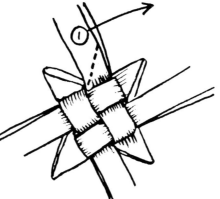

FIGURE 15.12

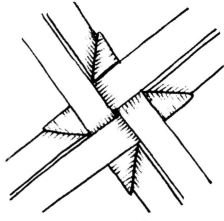

FIGURE 15.13

UNIT 16
Second star

This form is intermediate between the first and third stars.

Work the first star (unit 15) up to fig. 15.13 but do not cut off the ends of the strips. The work should look like fig. 16.1. The four points of the star hidden beneath the work are marked by dotted lines.

Strip 1 in fig. 16.1 is brought around and under the loop which lies beneath it as shown in fig. 16.2. The same side of the strip remains uppermost. Pull strip 1 through, as indicated by the arrow, until it will come no further. Flatten the loop that has been formed. The work should now look like fig. 16.3.

Treat strips 2, 3 and 4 in fig. 16.3 in the same manner as indicated by the arrows in fig. 16.4.

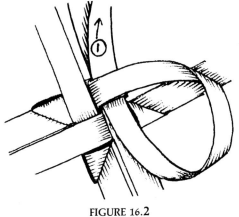

FIGURE 16.2

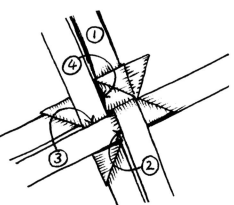

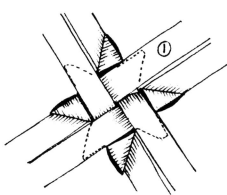

FIGURE 16.1

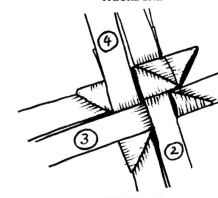

FIGURE 16.3

FIGURE 16.4

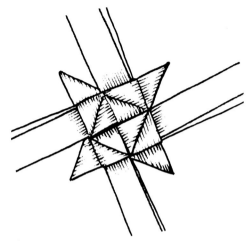

FIGURE 16.5

The work should now look like fig. 16.5.

Turn the work over and work the four strips on the other side in the same manner. Cut off the ends of all the strips and the star is complete.

This star, traditionally made from the creamy, immature leaves of the coconut palm, was taught to me by Robinson Fiuarua from a village near Auki on Malaita in the Solomon Islands. In the Areare area of the same island I also saw it used by children to carry coins to present at a feast held in honour of a deceased relative. When the adults presented their strings of traditional shell money carried attached to the tops of long saplings, the children carried up their coconut leaf toys containing their donations.

Work the first star (unit 15), following the diagrams up to fig. 15.13, but do

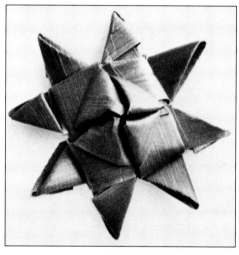

not cut off the ends of the strips. The work should look like fig. 17.1.

The movements are similar to those already worked for the second star (unit 16). The difference is that when strip 1 in fig. 17.1 is lifted and taken back through the loop that lies beneath it, the surface of the strip is changed. Examine fig. 17.2 closely. Pull the strip through slowly and carefully. The strip will buckle at the centre of the medallion as it is tightened, and this forms a raised point, heightening the three-dimensional effect of the finished star.

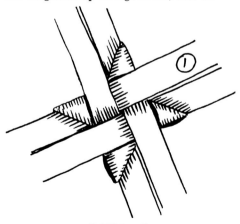

FIGURE 17.1

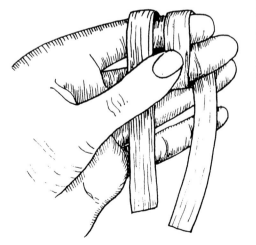

FIGURE 17.2

Work strips 2, 3 and 4 in fig. 17.2 in the same manner. Then cut off the waste ends and the star is complete.

In the star I first saw, one side of it was made in the form of the second star, leaving a flat side to wear against the chest as a medallion; the other side was as for the third star. To use as a Christmas tree decoration, both sides may be made in the manner of the third star.

UNIT 18
Fish

This is a traditional palm leaf toy from Thailand. It is also seen in synthetic materials in mobiles imported from South-east Asia.

Prepare two strips of flax leaf about 30 cm long and 1 cm wide. Take one of the strips and wrap it around the first and second fingers of the left hand as shown in fig. 18.1.

Remove from the fingers. You have now formed a double loop as in fig. 18.2.

FIGURE 18.1

FIGURE 18.2

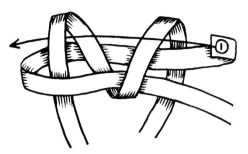

FIGURE 18.3

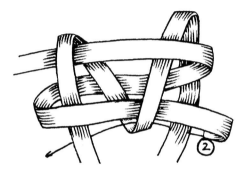

FIGURE 18.4

FIGURE 18.5

The second strip is threaded through the first in the manner shown in fig. 18.3.

The same strip 1 in fig. 18.3 is brought across and through the front of the knot, as indicated by the arrow, to lie in the position shown in fig. 18.4.

Strip 2 in fig. 18.4 is taken behind and through the back of the knot, as indicated by the arrow, to lie in the position shown in fig. 18.5.

The knot is gently tightened by pulling on all the strips, as indicated by the arrows in fig. 18.5. Do not pull it too tight at this stage. The knot should now look like fig. 18.6. The fins and tail may be trimmed at this stage for a simple version (fig. 18.7).

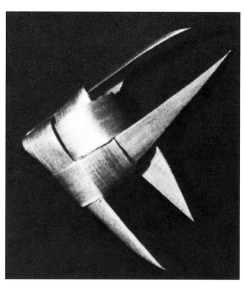

FIGURE 18.7

To continue for the complex form, turn the knot over to the position shown in fig. 18.8.

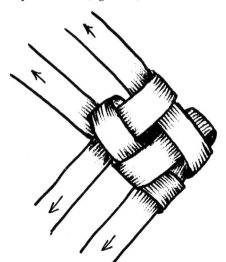

FIGURE 18.6

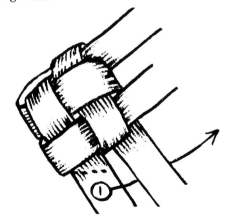

FIGURE 18.8

Strip 1 in fig. 18.8 is folded *back* and under the strip next to it to lie in the position shown in fig. 18.9.

Strip 1 in fig. 18.9 is folded *forward* and down over the two strips next to it, as indicated by the arrow, to lie in the position shown in fig. 18.10.

Strip 1 in fig 18.10 is folded along the dotted line, in the direction indicated by the arrow, to lie in the position shown in fig. 18.11.

Strip 1 in fig. 18.11 is brought up in the direction indicated by the arrow. It is taken under the strip marked 2. This may require some manipulation. The knot should now look like fig. 18.12.

Turn the knot over to the position shown in fig. 18.13.

FIGURE 18.9

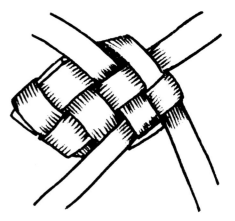

FIGURE 18.12

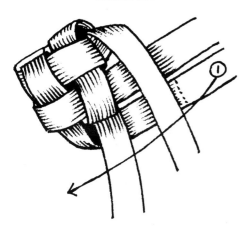

FIGURE 18.10

FIGURE 18.11

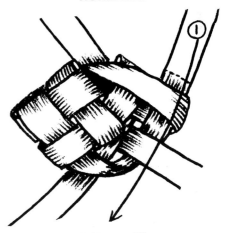

FIGURE 18.13

Strip 1 in fig. 18.13 is folded along the dotted line, in the direction indicated by the arrow, to lie in the position shown in fig. 18.14.

Strip 1 in fig. 18.14 is folded along the dotted line and in the direction indicated by the arrow. It is taken beneath the strip labelled 2. Again this may take some manipulation. The work should now look like fig. 18.15.

Two additional strips of flax about 7 cm long are inserted into the work in the positions indicated by the arrows. These are the tail. The fins and tail are now trimmed to shape, and when the flax is dry a spot of glue is added to each of the tail pieces to hold them in place. The fish is now complete.

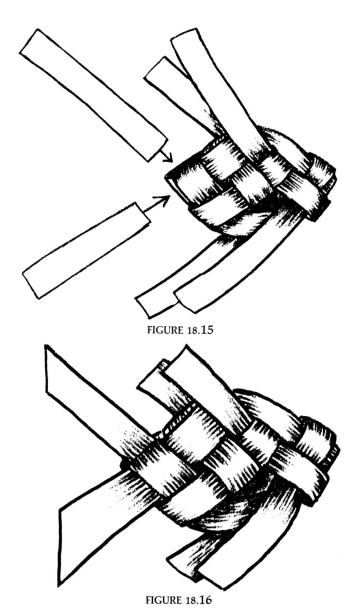

FIGURE 18.15

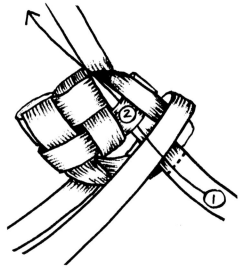

FIGURE 18.14

FIGURE 18.16

U N I T   1 9
Heron

The heron is a simple extension of the fish (unit 18) already described. The lower fins of the fish are left longer to form the legs of the heron, and the upper fins become the wings. The neck and head are made with an additional strip of flax the same width as that used for the body. Tie a knot in the strip and press it flat. This will be the head. Cut the beak to shape and the neck to the correct length. The bottom of the neck is then inserted into the plait of the body. Blu-tack can be added to hold it in place.

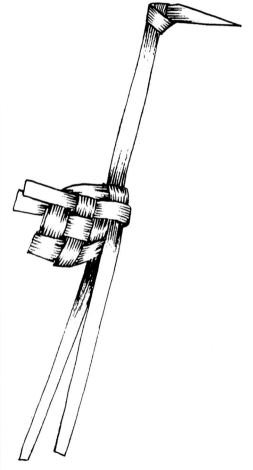

First bird

This toy bird, traditionally made of immature coconut leaflets, was shown to me by Frank Takotile of Guadalcanal in the Solomon Islands in 1971. A Hawaiian craft demonstrator at the South Pacific Arts Festival at Rotorua in 1976 made a similar bird.

Prepare two strips of flax about 2 cm wide and 60 cm long. With a ball-point pen, mark the ends of one strip of flax 1A and 1B (to make the directions below easier to follow). Mark the ends of the other strip 2A and 2B.

Make a loop in strip 1 as shown in fig. 20.1. Make sure that the ends 1A and 1B are in the positions shown. The loop is about 6 cm long.

The second strip is threaded through the loop from the back. The end marked 2B passes under the end marked 1B, as shown in fig. 20.2.

2B in fig. 20.2 is brought over 1A, then under the loop (but over 2A), then over 1B, as indicated by the arrow, to lie in the position shown in fig. 20.3.

1B is lifted and brought through the original loop, as indicated by the arrow in fig. 20.3, to lie in the position shown in fig. 20.4.

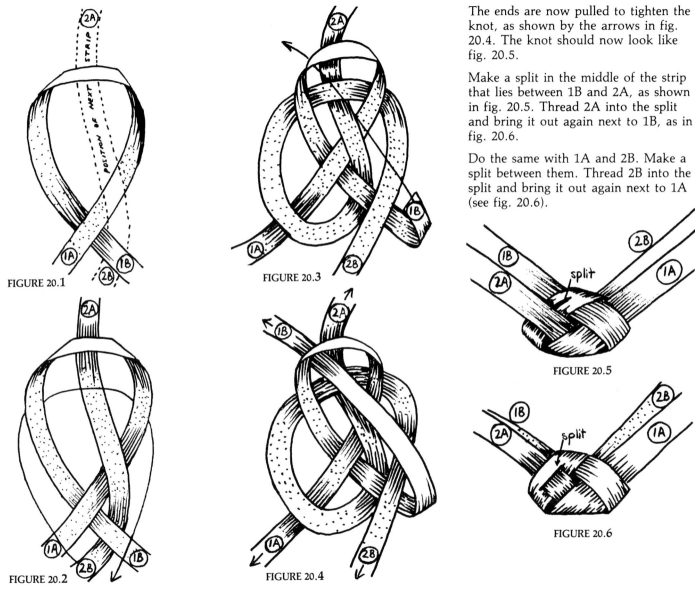

FIGURE 20.1

FIGURE 20.2

FIGURE 20.3

FIGURE 20.4

The ends are now pulled to tighten the knot, as shown by the arrows in fig. 20.4. The knot should now look like fig. 20.5.

Make a split in the middle of the strip that lies between 1B and 2A, as shown in fig. 20.5. Thread 2A into the split and bring it out again next to 1B, as in fig. 20.6.

Do the same with 1A and 2B. Make a split between them. Thread 2B into the split and bring it out again next to 1A (see fig. 20.6).

FIGURE 20.5

FIGURE 20.6

Fold 1A back on itself and thread it through, as shown by the arrow in fig. 20.7, to lie in the position shown in fig. 20.8. Do the same with 2B. It will pass under only half of the strip because of the split. The work should now look like fig. 20.8.

Trim the ends of 1A and 2B as shown in fig. 20.9. These are the wings.

1B and 2A are trimmed to form the tail. Many variations of length and shape may be made here. The ends of the tail can be twisted or scraped with a knife to make them curl (fig. 20.12).

Another strip of leaf is threaded through the two loops that form the neck and becomes the beak (see fig. 20.9). Trim the beak to shape as in fig. 20.10.

A small amount of Blu-tack will hold the beak in place; or when the flax is dry, a drop of glue may be added.

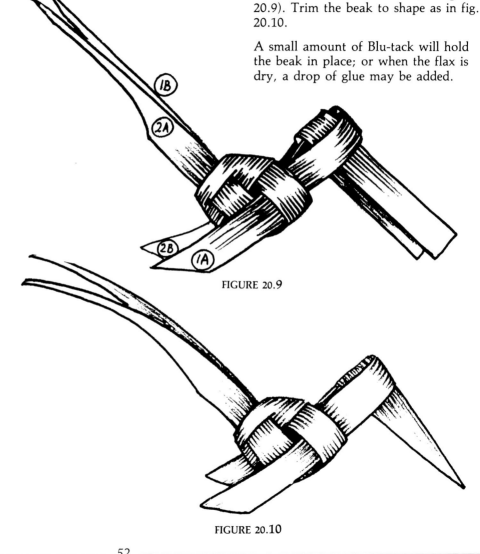

FIGURE 20.9

FIGURE 20.10

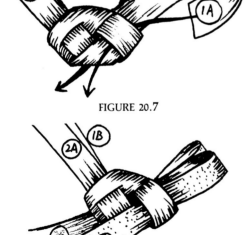

FIGURE 20.7

FIGURE 20.8

Clamp with a paper clip or clothes peg while it dries. The bird can be suspended by threading a narrow strip of flax through the back with a large needle.

Fig. 20.12 shows a variation in which the wings are brought around in a circle and threaded through the loops a second time, to make a bird of paradise.

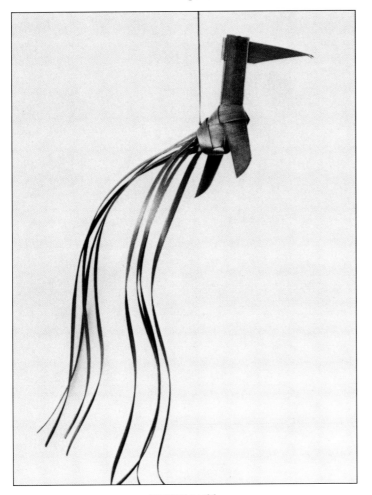

FIGURE 20.11

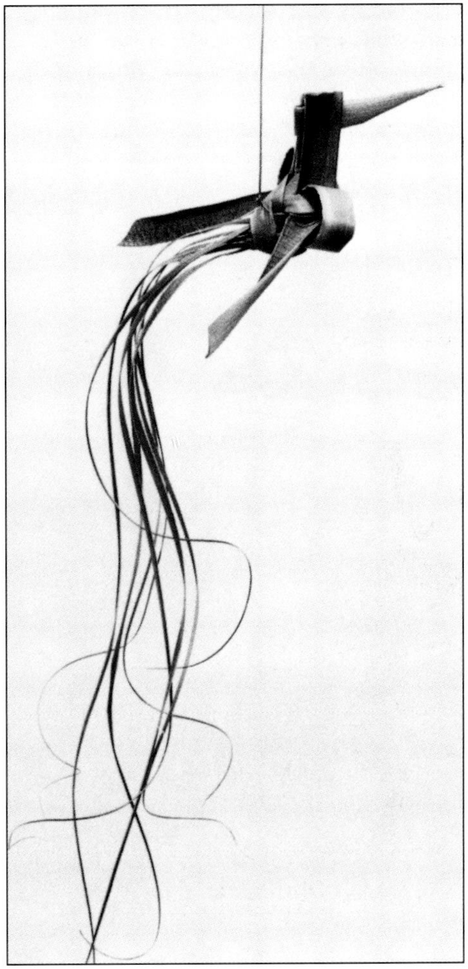

FIGURE 20.12

Figs. 20.13 and 20.14 show a similar bird copied from a specimen in the collection of the Auckland Museum. It is possibly from Vanuatu. An additional but smaller knot has been made in the same way and used as the head. The strips at the base of the neck fit into the body and protrude beneath to form the wings.

FIGURE 20.14

FIGURE 20.13

UNIT 21
Second bird

This toy was taught me by Mrs Emily Schuster of the Māori Art and Craft Institute, Rotorua 1980.

Prepare two strips of flax about 2 cm wide and 35 cm long. Split each strip into four, leaving the new strips joined for a length of about 10 cm, as in fig. 21.1.

Plait the two groups of strips as shown in fig. 21.2. Make sure that the strips cross above and below the intersecting strips in the same places as they do in fig. 21.2.

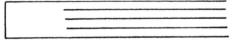

FIGURE 21.1

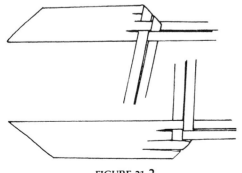

FIGURE 21.2

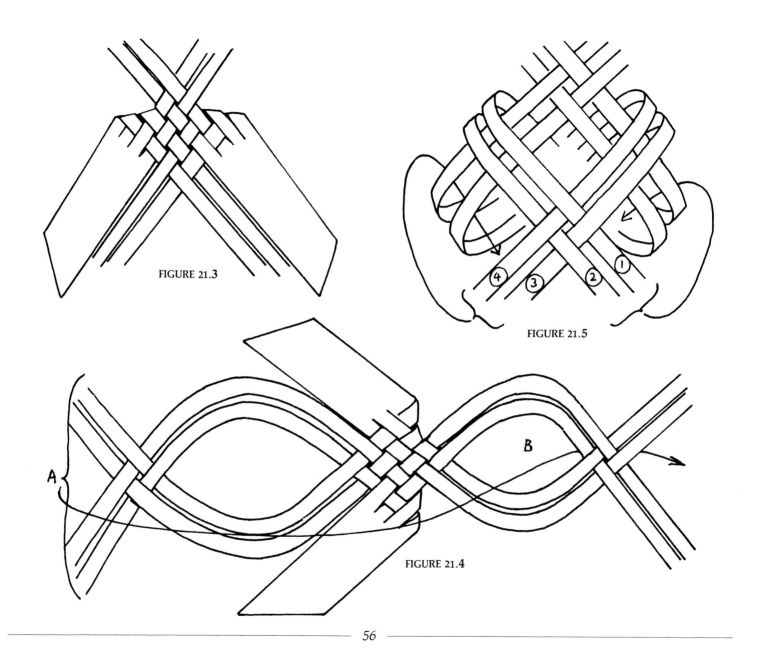

FIGURE 21.3

FIGURE 21.5

FIGURE 21.4

Now bring the two groups together and plait them as shown in fig. 21.3.

The four strips projecting above are plaited together again as shown in fig. 21.4. Hold them in place with a paper clip or a clothes peg. Treat the four strips projecting below in the same way.

The strips behind the wings labelled A in fig. 21.4 are brought through the opening labelled B in front of the wings to the positions shown in fig. 21.5.

Strips 1 and 2 in fig. 21.5 are brought around and through the loop, as indicated by the arrow.

Strips 3 and 4 are treated in the same way.

The work is now gently tightened by pulling on the strips individually.

Cut the wings and tail to the desired shape and length.

The four strips projecting in front of the wings are held together and tied with an overhand knot to form the head. Trim the beak to shape.

U N I T   2 2
Mosquito

This is a very simple but amusing balancing toy, shown to me by William Kisu of Malaita Island in the Solomons, 1971. It is traditionally made from immature coconut leaflets. Because the coconut leaf is lighter and thinner than flax, a thin, light leaf of flax should be selected.

Cut a small rectangle of flax leaf about 4 cm long and 1 to 1.5 cm wide. With a sharp pointed knife, lift a narrow strip from the surface of the leaf as shown in fig. 22.1.

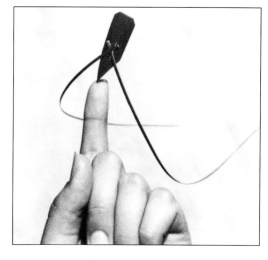

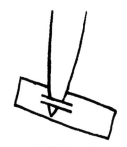

FIGURE 22.1

Cut the rectangle to the shape shown in fig. 22.2. Then tear two narrow strips of flax leaf about 20 cm long, scrape them lightly, and insert them into the slit in the positions shown in fig. 22.2

The toy is balanced on the finger tip.

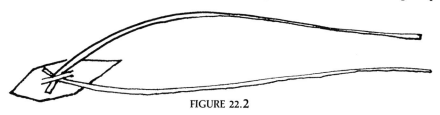

FIGURE 22.2

UNIT 23
Reindeer

Scandinavians make traditional Christmas decorations of straw, and this reindeer is one of them. It is also made of palmetto in Central America.

Prepare five strips of flax about 60 to 80 cm long and about 1 cm wide.

Lay strip 1, which will form the tail, on a flat surface. Place the next two strips as shown in fig. 23.1.

Add two more strips in the positions shown in fig 23.2. Fold strip 2 along the dotted lines and plait both ends under and over the other strips, as indicated by the arrows, to lie in the positions shown in fig. 23.3.

Strips 1 and 2 in fig. 23.3 will remain where they are to form the hind legs of the deer. Fold strips 3 and 4 along the dotted lines and plait back into the body of the work to lie in the positions shown in fig. 23.4.

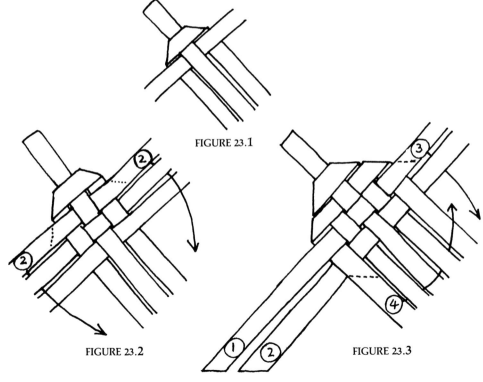

FIGURE 23.1

FIGURE 23.2

FIGURE 23.3

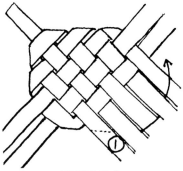

FIGURE 23.4

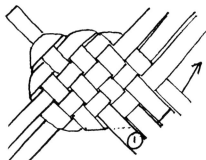

FIGURE 23.5

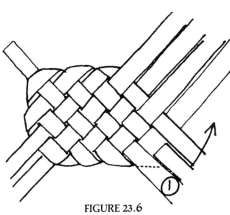

FIGURE 23.6

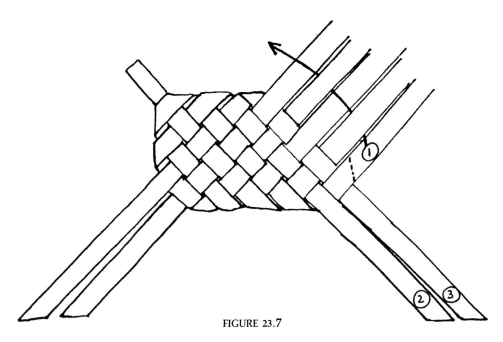

FIGURE 23.7

Fold strip 1 in fig. 23.4 along the dotted line and plait back into the body of the work, as indicated by the arrow, to lie in the position shown in fig. 23.5.

Fold strip 1 in fig. 23.5 along the dotted line and plait back into the body of the work, as indicated by the arrow, to lie in the position shown in fig. 23.6.

Fold strip 1 in fig. 23.6 along the dotted line and plait back into the body of the work, as indicated by the arrow, to lie in the position shown in fig. 23.7.

Fold strip 1 in fig. 23.7 along the dotted line and plait back into the body of the work. Strips 2 and 3 remain where they are to form the front legs of the deer.

Fold strip 1 in fig. 23.8 along the dotted line and plait back into the body of the work.

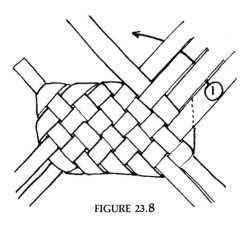

FIGURE 23.8

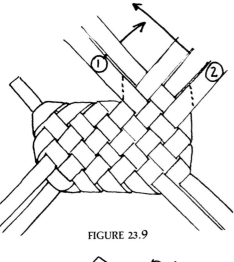

FIGURE 23.9

Fold strip 2 in fig. 23.9 along the dotted line and plait back into the body of the work. Fold strip 1 along the dotted line and plait back into the work. Repeat the movements shown in fig. 23.9 until the neck is long enough.

Fold strip 1 in fig. 23.10 along the dotted line and plait back into the work. Strip 2 is left where it is and becomes the ear of the deer.

Fold strip 1 in fig. 23.11 along the dotted line and plait back into the work as indicated.

Fold strips 1 and 2 in fig. 23.12 along the dotted lines and plait back into the body of the work as indicated.

Fold strip 1 in fig. 23.13 back on itself, along the dotted line, and plait back into the work as indicated. Treat strip 2 in the same way. Turn the work over and plait the two remaining strips back into the work in a similar manner. The work should now look like fig. 23.14.

For the reindeer antlers, two small strips of flax can be folded concertina fashion (fig. 23.15) and inserted near the ears.

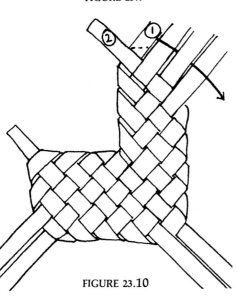

FIGURE 23.10

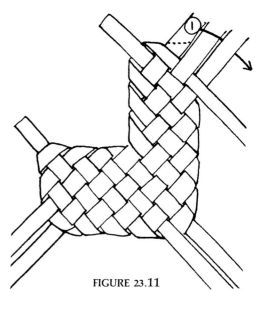

FIGURE 23.11

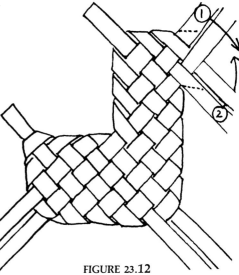

FIGURE 23.12

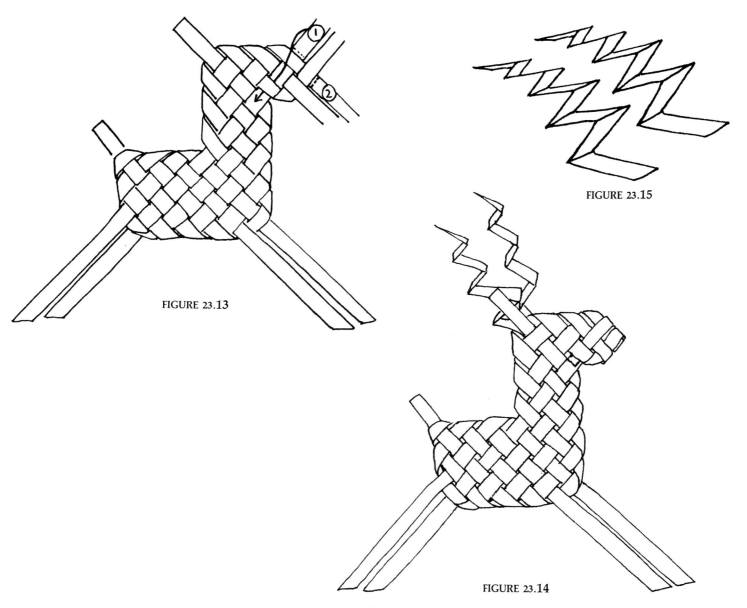

FIGURE 23.13

FIGURE 23.15

FIGURE 23.14

UNIT 24
Giraffe and dachshund

These are variations on the reindeer (unit 23). Lengthening the neck and legs creates a giraffe; lengthening the body, a dachshund. Other animals can be made in the same way by altering the proportions of the various parts of the body.

For the giraffe, work as for the reindeer until the neck is reached (fig. 23.9) and simply repeat the movements indicated by the arrows until the neck is long enough. The head is made as for the reindeer.

The dachshund is also made following the diagrams for the reindeer. Work unit 23 up to fig. 23.4. Then work fig. 24.1 below.

Strip 1 in fig. 24.1 is folded along the dotted line, in the direction indicated by the arrow, and plaited back into the body of the work. Strip 2 is folded along the dotted line, in the direction indicated by the arrow, and plaited back into the body of the work. Continue to repeat these movements until the body of the dog is long enough. Follow the rest of the diagrams for the reindeer (unit 23) but make the neck a bit shorter.

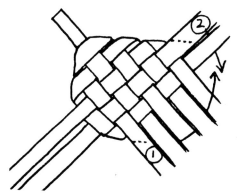

FIGURE 24.1

UNIT 25
Caterpillar

Children enjoy making this simple caterpillar or centipede using the push-and-pull braid.

Prepare a strip of flax about 2 cm wide and as long as possible. Split the strip in half but leave about 6 cm joined together at one end. If the two strips split apart they can be tied together with a strip of flax.

Fold strip 2 in fig. 25.1 back towards you to lie in the position shown. Fold strip 1 along the dotted line, in the direction indicated by the arrow, to lie in the position shown in fig. 25.2.

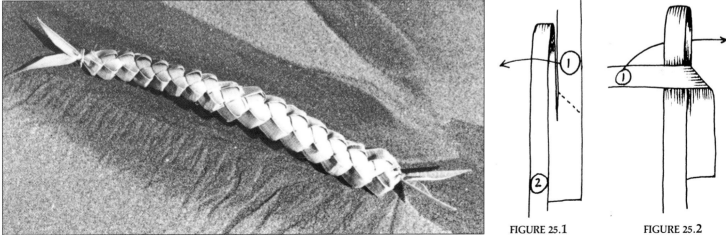

FIGURE 25.1   **FIGURE 25.2**

Bring the same strip around behind the work as indicated by the arrow in fig. 25.2 to lie in the position shown in fig. 25.3.

Bend the flax as shown in fig. 25.3. This loop 1 is pushed through the loop labelled 2, as indicated by the arrow, to lie in the position shown in fig. 25.4.

Pull on strip 2 in fig. 25.4 until the loop is tight, as shown in fig. 25.5.

Make a loop in strip 2, as shown in fig. 25.5, and push this loop through the loop labelled 1. Pull the end of strip 1 to tighten the loop. Continue to work figs. 25.3, 25.4 and 25.5 until the plait is long enough.

Plait the full length of two strips, then tie off the ends with fine strips of flax. The butt ends of the strips can be cut and folded back to represent feelers or simply cut to points as strings.

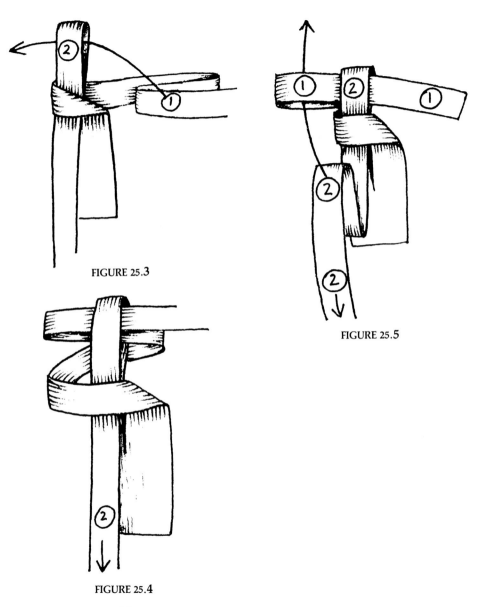

FIGURE 25.3

FIGURE 25.5

FIGURE 25.4

U N I T 2 6
Snake

This moving snake delights small children.

Prepare two strips of flax about 1.5 cm wide and as long as possible. Tie them firmly together at the butt ends with a narrow strip of flax, as in fig. 26.1.

Twist one strip so that it lies at right angles to the other strip as in fig. 26.2.

Strip 1 in fig. 26.2 is folded along the dotted line and in the direction indicated by the arrow to lie in the position shown in fig. 26.3.

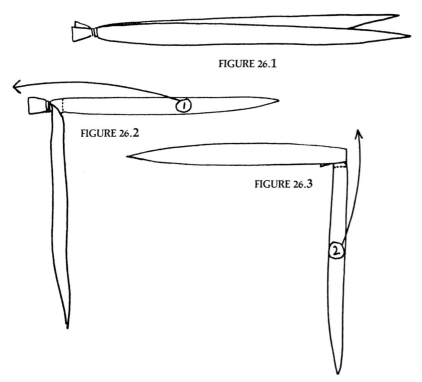

FIGURE 26.1

FIGURE 26.2

FIGURE 26.3

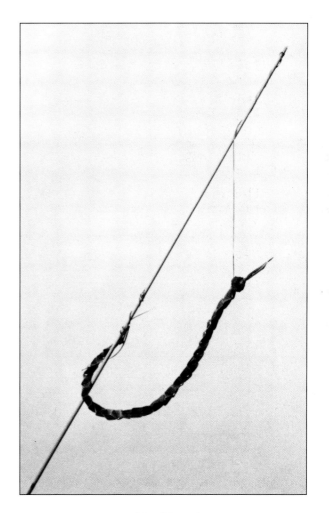

Strip 2 in fig. 26.3 is folded along the dotted line and moved in the direction indicated by the arrow to lie in the position shown in fig. 26.4.

Strip 1 in fig. 26.4 is folded along the dotted line and in the direction indicated by the arrow to lie in the position shown in fig. 26.5.

Strip 2 in fig. 26.5 is folded along the dotted line and moved in the direction indicated by the arrow to lie in the position shown in fig. 26.6.

Strip 1 in fig. 26.6 is folded along the dotted line and moved in the direction indicated by the arrow to lie in the position shown in fig. 26.3. Continue to repeat the movements shown in figs. 26.3 to 26.6 until all the flax has been used.

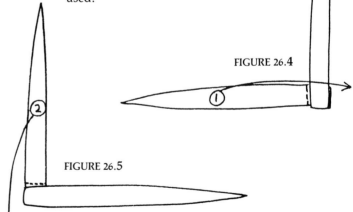

FIGURE 26.4

FIGURE 26.5

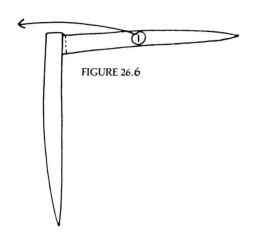

FIGURE 26.6

To make the snake, treat the heavier butt end of the finished braid as the head and cut the butt ends to the shape of fangs. Tie the snake's head to a narrow strip of flax about 30 cm long and attach the other end to the end of a 60 cm stick. Weight the head of the snake by tying a small stone to it or by thrusting it through a metal nut as in the photograph. The tail end of the snake is tied to the middle of the stick. When the stick is moved with a downward motion, the weight on the head causes it to dart forward in a realistic, snake-like manner.

UNIT 27
Three-ply braid

Most readers will know this, the commonest braid, but it is included here for those who do not. It may be used to make the pāua shell stilts (unit 30).

Prepare three strips of flax about 1 cm wide and as long as possible and tie them together. Secure this end to something firm or ask someone else to hold it. Spread out the three strips into a fan as shown in fig. 27.1. For this braid the shiny side of the strips may be kept uppermost at all times or, alternatively, the strips may be turned over at each movement (see photograph).

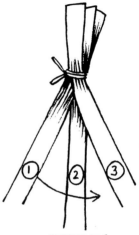

FIGURE 27.1

FIGURE 27.2

Bring the left-hand strip 1 over the middle strip 2, as indicated by the arrow in fig. 27.1, to become the new middle strip.

Bring the right-hand strip 3 over the middle strip 1, as indicated by the arrow in fig. 27.2 to become the new middle strip.

Bring the left-hand strip 2 over the middle strip 3 in fig. 27.3.

Bring the right-hand strip 1 over the middle strip 2 in fig. 27.4.

Continue repeating the same movements, bringing the strip from the left to the centre, then the strip from the right to the centre.

FIGURE 27.3

FIGURE 27.4

U N I T 2 8
Five-ply braid

This simple braid is made in the same way as the three-ply braid (unit 27). In view of its attractiveness and simplicity, it is surprising that it is not more widely used.

Take five strips of prepared flax and tie them together at one end. The movements are the same as those already practised for the three-ply braid except that each outside strip passes over two strips instead of one to reach the centre of the braid. The shiny side of the strips may be kept uppermost or, alternatively, the strips turned over at each movement (see photograph).

Bring strip 1 in fig. 28.1 to the centre, passing over strips 3 and 2.

Bring strip 5 in fig. 28.2 to the centre, passing over strips 4 and 1. Continue to work the same movements following figs. 28.1 and 28.2. A seven-ply braid can be made in the same way.

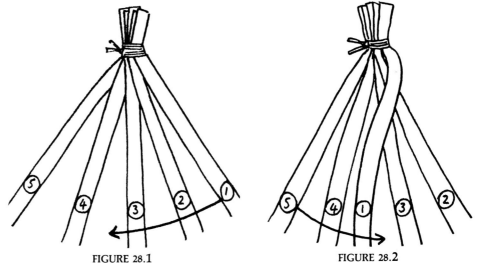

FIGURE 28.1   FIGURE 28.2

UNIT 29
Round four-ply braid

The attractive and well-known round braid, in which four working strips are used, may be used for kit handles or with the pāua shell stilts (unit 30).

Prepare four strips of flax about 1 cm wide and as long as possible and tie them together at one end. Spread the strips into a fan as in fig. 29.1. Normally this braid is worked with the shiny surface on the outside.

Lift strip 2 in fig. 29.1 and take it over strip 3, as indicated by the arrow.

Put the right hand between strips 2 and 4 in fig. 29.2 to reach behind for strip 1. Bring strip 1 to the front between strips 2 and 4 and take it over strip 2, as indicated by the arrow.

Put the left hand between strips 3 and 1 in fig. 29.3 and reach behind for strip 4. Bring it to the front between strips 3 and 1 and take it over strip 1, as indicated by the arrow.

Put the right hand in between strips 2 and 4 in fig. 29.4 and reach behind for strip 3. Bring it to the front between strips 2 and 4 and take it over strip 4, as indicated by the arrow.

Put the left hand in between strips 1 and 3 in fig. 29.5 and reach behind for strip 2. Bring it to the front between strips 1 and 3 and take it over strip 3. Repeat the movements shown in figs. 29.4 and 29.5.

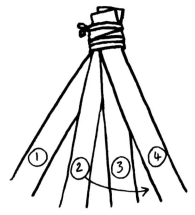

FIGURE 29.1

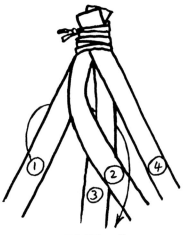

FIGURE 29.2

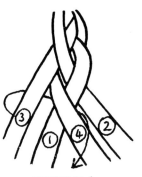

FIGURE 29.3

FIGURE 29.4

FIGURE 29.5

Pacific Island children play with stilts made by threading a length of cord through the eye of half a coconut shell. Each foot is placed on a half shell and the cord from each passes between the big toe and the second toe. Māori children used pāua shells for the same game, using strips of flax passed through the natural holes of the shells. It is not uncommon today to see children improvise with food cans.

The item is included here as an exercise to give practice in the three-ply braid (unit 27) or the round four-ply braid (unit 29). Use either of these for the cord and choose thick, strong shells.

Braid a three- or four-ply cord about two metres long. Push one end of the cord through one of the natural holes in the shell from the outside and tie in a large knot (or to a short stick) on the inside of the shell. Ths knot prevents the cord from pulling out. Attach the other end of the cord to the other shell in the same way.

To walk on the shells, the centre of the cord is held in the hand, and a foot placed on each shell with the cord running between the big and second toes on each foot. Alternatively, separate cords can be made for each shell.

UNIT 31
Flat four-ply braid

A simple four-ply braid, which could be used by children as a headband, is included here as a practice exercise for the ball sequence (units 33 to 36) and the four-ply snake (unit 32).

Prepare two strips of flax about 2 cm wide and split them down the centre, so that they remain joined only at the butt end as in fig. 31.1. If the flax tends to split right through, tie a fine strip around the end to hold it together.

Thread the strips through each other so that they lie in the positions shown in fig. 31.2. Make sure that the correct strips are on top and the others beneath or it will not be possible to follow the diagrams.

Fold strip 1 in fig. 31.2 along the dotted line, in the direction indicated by the arrow, to lie in the position shown in fig. 31.3. The underside of the strip is now uppermost.

FIGURE 31.1

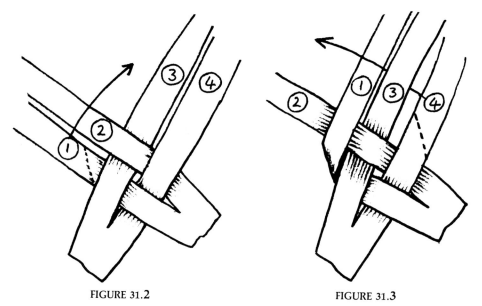

FIGURE 31.2   FIGURE 31.3

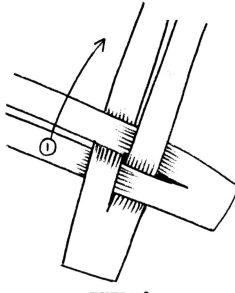

FIGURE 31.4

Fold strip 4 in fig. 31.3 along the dotted line, in the direction indicated by the arrow, to lie in the position shown in fig. 31.4. Again the surface of the strip is changed. Continue to make the movements shown in figs. 31.3 and 31.4 until the desired length has been reached. A new strip can be added by placing it on top of an old strip and plaiting the two strips together for a few movements. When the join is secure the ends can be cut off.

U N I T   3 2
Four-ply snake

This snake, shown to me by Henry Apato from Malaita Island in the Solomons, is made in exactly the same manner as the square ball that follows in unit 33 and is an excellent introduction to it. It is also an amusing ornament in itself. When hung in a draught by a thin thread it will revolve with a spiral motion.

Prepare two strips of flax about 2 or 3 cm wide and as long as possible. Split each strip down the centre, leaving them joined together at the butt end.

The snake is made in the same way as the flat four-ply braid (unit 31), except that the surface of the strips is not changed. The shiny upper side of the leaf remains uppermost at all times.

Thread the strips through each other so that they lie in the positions shown in fig. 32.2. Make sure that the correct strips are on top and the others beneath. The shiny surfaces are uppermost.

Move strip 1 in fig. 32.2 in the direction indicated by the arrow. Make sure that you *do not* change the surface of the leaf.

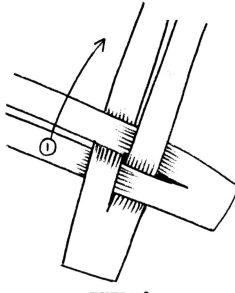

FIGURE 32.2

FIGURE 32.1

Move strip 1 in fig. 32.3 in the direction indicated by the arrow. Again, make sure that the shiny surface remains uppermost.

Move strip 1 in fig. 32.4 in the direction indicated by the arrow. As you work, press upwards from beneath with your fingers to curve the upper surface. Keep the work fairly tight. Continue in the same manner, plaiting alternately from one side and then from the other as in figs. 32.2 and 32.3. Allow the work to spiral to one side. Tie off the narrow ends with a thin strip of flax. Tie and trim the head to shape at the thick end. Attach a thin cord such as sewing cotton to the head to suspend the snake from the ceiling. If there is a draught it will revolve.

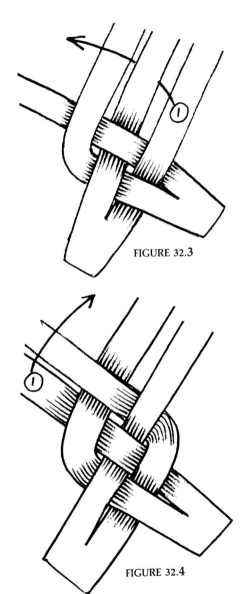

FIGURE 32.3

FIGURE 32.4

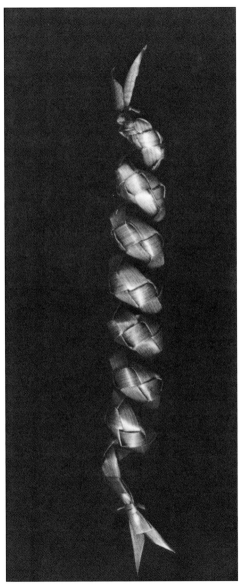

UNIT 33
Square ball

I was first taught how to make this ball by George Palua of Gela Island when he was at school at Maravovo on Guadalcanal in 1971. This leaf cube is well known and used as a ball on very many islands in the Pacific.

Prepare four strips of flax about 2 cm wide. Tie them together in pairs at the pointed ends, as in fig. 33.1.

Now follow the directions for making the four-ply snake (unit 32). Work quite tightly, allowing the work to curl up inside itself as it progresses.

As the ball forms, keep pressing the flat surfaces between the thumb and fingers. This helps to make the corners more pronounced. Once the cube becomes firm, the waste ends of the strips are each threaded along the path of the strip beneath until they are secure. The waste part is then cut off. Island children often put a small stone inside the ball if more weight is required for a game.

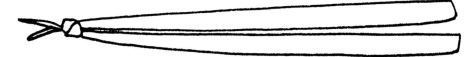

FIGURE 33.1

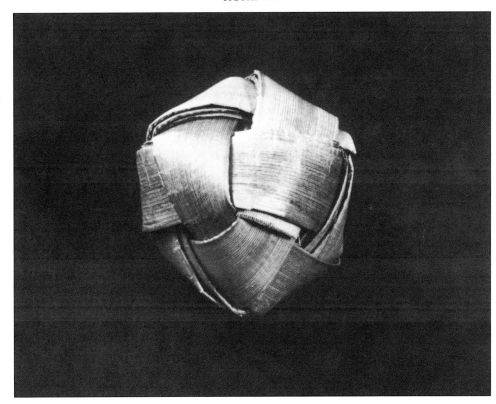

UNIT 34
Oblong ball

The oblong ball is made in exactly the same way as the square ball (unit 33) except that six strips are used instead of four. It is only slightly more difficult to hold. I learnt it from George Palua of Gela Island but it is also made on other islands in the Solomons and elsewhere in the Pacific.

Three double strips are required. Lay the strips out as shown in fig. 34.1. Strip 1 is plaited into the work from the left. The shiny surface of the leaf remains uppermost. Strip 2 is then plaited in from the right. Continue these movements until the ball is firm, and then plait in the ends and cut off the waste.

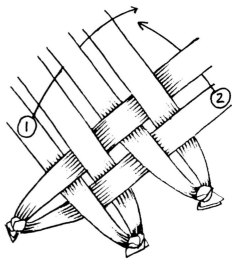

FIGURE 34.1

UNIT 35
Four-cornered triangular ball

This was invented by Selwyn Tafimae of Kwara'ae on Malaita in the Solomon Islands when he was experimenting with coconut leaflets in 1971. It is made by a method similar to those already described.

Prepare six strips of flax about 1.5 cm wide and tie them together in pairs at the pointed ends, as described for the other ball shapes. Plait the strips together so that they lie in the positions shown in fig. 35.1

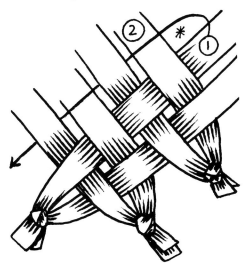

FIGURE 35.1

Strip 1 in fig. 35.1 is turned and plaited back alongside itself as indicated by the arrow. The shiny side of the strip remains uppermost. To make this movement, strip 2 will have to bend back to allow strip 1 to be placed in the correct position. The first corner will form at the point where strip 1 folds back over strip 2 (marked *).

Strip 3 in fig. 35.2 is moved in the direction indicated by the arrow to lie parallel to strip 1. Fig 35.3 shows the work diagrammatically only. There are no long loops in the work where strips 1 and 3 curve around, as it would seem from fig. 35.3. They are pulled tight until the corner forms.

There are now four strips pointing in one direction and two in the other, as was the case in fig. 35.1. The second corner is formed by plaiting strip 3 in

fig. 35.3 back alongside itself, as indicated by the arrow. The surface of the strip is not changed. Strip 1 is moved as indicated to lie parallel to strip 3. The second corner has now been formed. Again there are four strips pointing in one direction and two in the other.

The same movements are made for the third corner, following the directions given for fig. 35.2.

After the completion of each corner, two strips should point in one direction

and four in the other. And again, after each corner, the two strips are plaited back into the four as shown in figs. 35.2 and 35.3. Plait four corners altogether.

After the completion of the fourth corner the ends of the strips are plaited back into the work, each strip being placed along the top of the corresponding strip which lies beneath.

When the work is firm the waste ends are cut off.

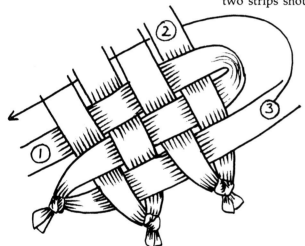

FIGURE 35.2

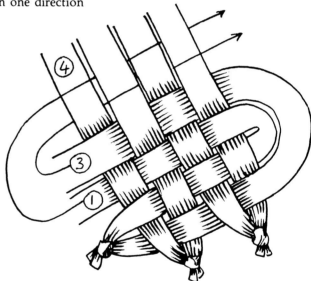

FIGURE 35.3

UNIT 36
Five-cornered triangular ball

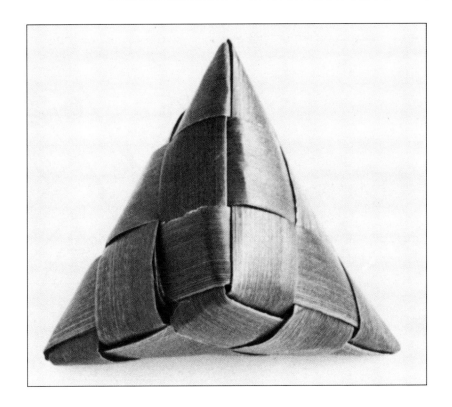

I discovered this shape myself while I was trying to remember how to make the four-cornered triangular ball (unit 35).

Prepare six strips of flax about 1.5 cm wide and tie them together in pairs as was done for the other balls. Plait the strips into one another so that they lie in the positions shown in fig. 36.1.

Strip 3 in fig. 36.1 is brought back alongside itself and plaited into strips 4, 5 and 6, as indicated by the arrow, to

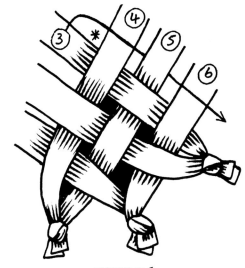

FIGURE 36.1

lie as shown in fig. 36.2. However, care must be taken to see that the same surface remains uppermost. This will force strip 4 out of line and buckle the work so that a corner will form at *, with its point pointing towards you.

In the same way, strip 4 in fig. 36.2 is brought back and plaited into strips 1 and 2. Again the same surface must

remain uppermost. The corner that has formed where strips 3 and 4 cross one another is a very pointed one.

Strips 1 and 2 in fig. 36.3 are now plaited into strips 5 and 6, and the first corner is complete. The working edge should now look like fig. 36.1, with three strips pointing in each direction.

Repeat the movements for figs. 36.1, 36.2 and 36.3, and the second corner will be formed. The third corner is made in the same way. A fourth corner can now be plaited over the top of the first one.

The loose ends of the flax are plaited into the corresponding strips beneath and the waste cut off.

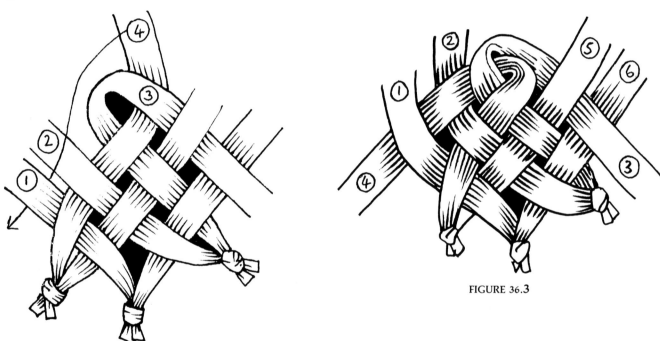

FIGURE 36.2

FIGURE 36.3

UNIT 37
Camera

This is a popular toy with the children of Tikopia, who make it from coconut leaflets and use it to play at taking photos of one another, holding it to the eye and pressing a finger on the top to "click" it as they have seen visitors to their island do. There it is called tilotilo. It was shown to me by Hosea Fenauta on Tikopia in 1975.

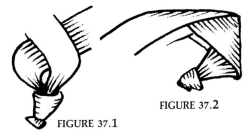

FIGURE 37.1
FIGURE 37.2

The right-hand strip is taken over the other strip, without changing the surface of either strip (fig. 37.1).

Again without changing the surface of either strip (the shiny surface is on the outside of the toy at all times), take the right-hand strip over the other strip. Because the surfaces of the strips do not change, the leaves will have to buckle, forming corners. Fig. 37.2 shows the work from the side.

Continue to plait the right-hand strip over the other strip without changing the surface. The work will proceed around the centre of the knot in the same way as the square ball (unit 33). Each movement will form a new corner. After the fourth corner, the subsequent corners will be around those already formed. As the strips of flax near the end, plait them back into the work and cut off the waste ends.

Prepare two strips of flax about 1.5 cm wide and tie them together near the pointed tips with an overhand knot. If the knot is tied too near the tips the strips will be too thin to work with. Cut off the pointed ends. There is only one movement used for the whole toy. However, because it is not a flat plait it is difficult to show in a diagram.

UNIT 38
Another square ball

This ball is made on many islands in the Pacific. I first saw it on Malaita in the Solomon Islands.

Prepare six strips of flax about 40 cm long and 1.5 cm wide. Tie them together in pairs at the thin end. Interlace the pairs of strips as shown in fig. 38.1.

The first corner is formed between the centre two of the four parallel strips.

FIGURE 38.1

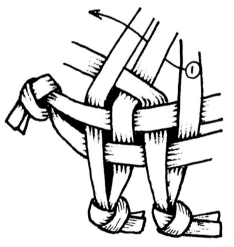

FIGURE 38.2

Move strip 1 in fig. 38.1 in the direction indicated by the arrow to the position shown in fig. 38.2.

Move strip 1 in fig. 38.2 in the direction indicated by the arrow to the position shown in fig. 38.3.

Turn the work around so that the four parallel strips are pointing away, as in fig. 38.4.

The second corner is formed following the same sequence. First move strip 1 in fig. 38.4 to the position indicated by the arrow. Complete the corner by following the movements shown in fig. 38.2. The knots that tie the strips in pairs are pushed inside the ball as the work progresses.

Subsequent corners are formed in the same way, always forming the next corner between the centre two of the four parallel strips. When the ball is fully formed, tuck the ends of the strips into the ball along the top of the strip that lies beneath and then cut off the waste.

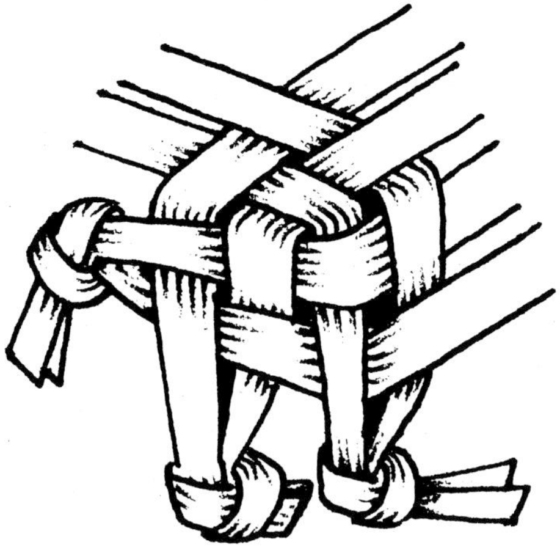

UNIT 39
Kiribati ball

FIGURE 38.3

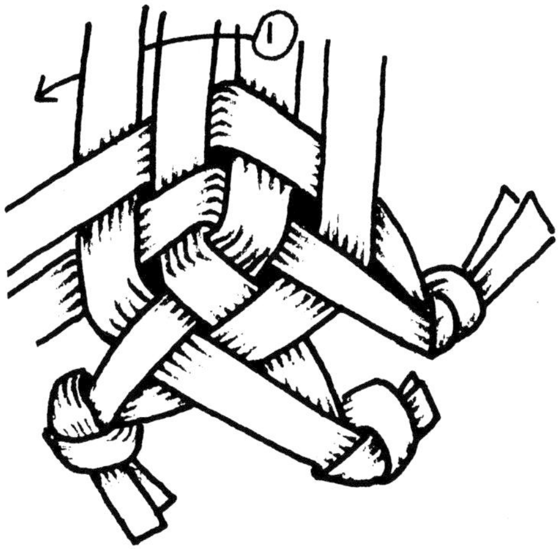

FIGURE 38.4

I was shown how to make this ball by Tauni Tioon, originally from Kiribati but teaching at Goldie College near Munda in the Solomon Islands in 1971. It is made from coconut leaflets, and a group of Kiribati pupils at the school demonstrated a game in which the ball was passed around a circle by kicking it with various parts of the foot in time to a song chanted by the players and onlookers. They were very adept at keeping the ball in motion without dropping it. An identical ball is made in Tuvalu.

Prepare twelve strips of flax about 1.5 cm wide. Tie them together in pairs at the narrow, pointed ends of the strips but not too near the end (fig. 39.1). At the point where they are tied they should be almost as wide as they will be at their full width. Cut off the pointed ends.

Take two pairs of strips and plait them together so that they lie in the positions shown in fig. 39.2. Make certain that the correct strips are on top and the rest beneath.

FIGURE 39.2

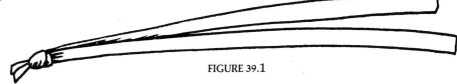

FIGURE 39.1

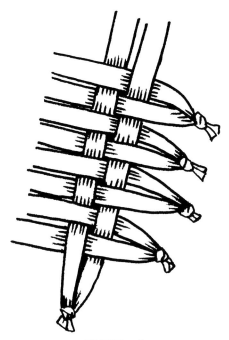

FIGURE 39.3

Add three more pairs of strips, as shown in fig. 39.3.

Add the final pair of strips in the position shown in fig. 39.4. Strips 1 and 2 are plaited, in the directions indicated by the arrows, the same surface remaining uppermost. The first corner of the ball will be formed between strips 1 and 2. Fig. 39.5 shows the corner in diagrammatic form only.

Strips 1, 2 and 3 are now plaited into strips 4, 5 and 6, as in fig. 39.5, to look like fig. 39.6.

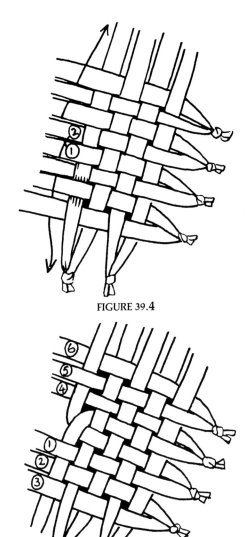

FIGURE 39.4

FIGURE 39.5

There are now eight working strips along one side and four along the other. The next corner is formed at the point marked * in fig. 39.6. Strips 1, 2, 3 and 4 are plaited into strips 5, 6, 7 and 8.

Continue the work in the same way. After each set of movements there will be eight working strips on one side and four on the other. The next movement is always at the centre of the eight strips. Once the ball is well formed, the ends of the strips are tucked into the body of the work and trimmed, as was done with all the other balls.

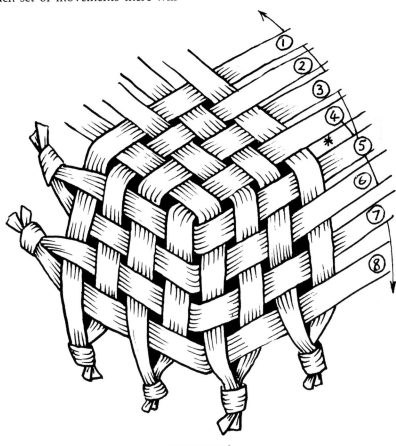

FIGURE 39.6

UNIT 40
Poro whā (Māori flax ball)

Examples of this children's toy may be seen in the Auckland War Memorial Museum and in the National Museum, Wellington. Very little is known of their antiquity or the games associated with them.

Prepare four strips of flax leaf about 3 cm wide and split each almost to the butt end. If they tend to split right through they may be secured by tying a narrow strip around each or by folding them transversely near the butt, as

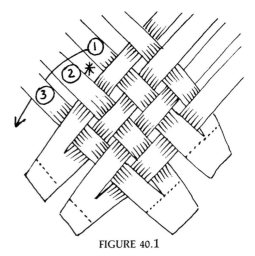

FIGURE 40.1

shown by the dotted lines in fig. 40.1

Move strip 1 in fig. 40.1 in the direction indicated by the arrow to lie in the position shown in fig. 40.2. The strip is not folded and the same surface remains uppermost. Strips 2 and 3 will tend to move to the right and the corner will begin to form at the point marked *.

Move strip 2 in fig. 40.2 in the direction indicated by the arrow to the position shown in fig. 40.3. Again the same surface remains uppermost. The first corner is now formed.

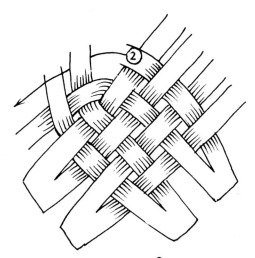

FIGURE 40.2

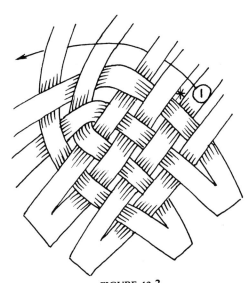

FIGURE 40.3

Move strip 1 in fig. 40.3 in the direction indicated by the arrow to the position shown in fig. 40.4. The second corner will begin to form at the point marked *.

Move strip 1 in fig. 40.4 in the direction indicated by the arrow to the position shown in fig. 40.5. The second corner has now been formed.

Move strip 1 in fig. 40.5 in the direction indicated by the arrow to form a new corner at the point marked *. This is the same movement already used in fig. 40.1. The next movement (strip 2 in fig. 40.5) is the same as that in fig. 40.2.

In the same way, work again the movements shown in figs. 40.3 and 40.4.

Continue to work these movements following figs. 40.1 to 40.4. The butt ends are pushed into the centre of the ball as it forms around them. When the cube is completely formed, with a total eight corners, the waste ends are threaded through the work, each on top of and following the path of the strip beneath it. When the ball is secure the waste ends are simply cut off.

The same toy is made from coconut leaf by children of the Roviana-speaking area of Western Province in the Solomon Islands.

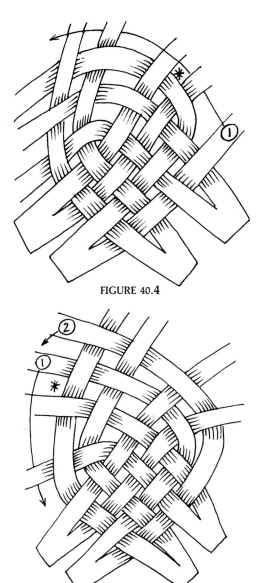

FIGURE 40.4

FIGURE 40.5

UNIT 41
Cup

This flax leaf cup was shown to me by Mrs Monica Isherwood (née Pourini) of Turangi, who played with them as a child but remembers no special name associated with them. The same toy was made from coconut leaflets by boys at Maravovo School on Guadalcanal in the Solomon Islands in 1970, but they called it a basket.

W.J. Phillipps (1954) describes full-sized flax drinking cups called konenewai, used in the southern parts of the South Island and Stewart Island. These were made of half of a young flax leaf (rito).

Prepare a single strip of flax about 3 cm wide. The strip of flax is wrapped around the first two fingers of the left hand, beginning with the butt end of the leaf. Once the circle of leaf has been formed, it is removed from the fingers and more rounds wrapped around in a spiral as in fig. 41.1.

When the roll is 3 or 4 cm long flatten it at the point marked * in fig. 41.1.

Now bring strip 1 across the end of the roll, closing it, and begin to circle the roll in the opposite direction as shown in fig. 41.2.

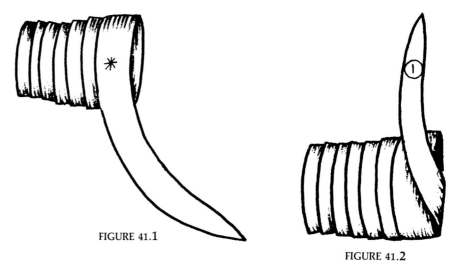

FIGURE 41.1

FIGURE 41.2

When it reaches the other flattened side cross it over the now closed bottom again, as shown in fig. 41.3.

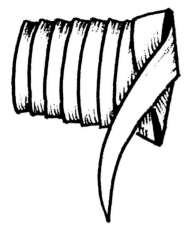

FIGURE 41.3

Make several more movements in this manner until the base is securely closed and thread the end of strip 1 through one of the final rounds to hold it in place. This is called the handle of the cup by Māori children but in the Solomon Islands the tail is cut off and the toy called a basket.

UNIT 42
First puzzle

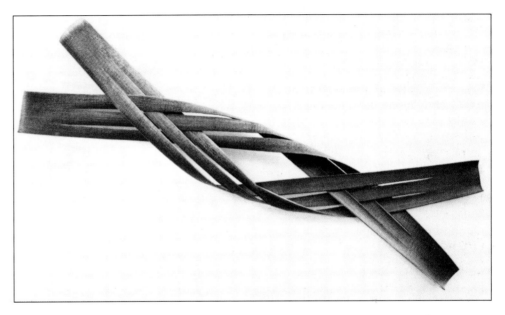

Puzzles made from coconut leaf are widely distributed throughout the Pacific Islands. Puzzle 1, for which the directions are given, was shown to me by Rodock Kotulegu of Ysabel Island in the Solomons in 1971. It is also known on Malaita. It is traditionally made from a young coconut leaflet but can also be made from New Zealand flax. The aim of the game is to unravel it without splitting the flax. This is difficult if the method of construction has not been observed, so keep it a secret!

Prepare two strips of flax about 3 cm wide and 15 cm long. The flax used should be flexible and not too inclined to split. Place the two strips on top of one another and with the thumbnail make two slits in each piece of flax as is shown in fig. 42.1. The slits are made through both strips but must not be made right to the ends of the strips.

With the forefinger of the left hand, pick up the first strip from the leaf beneath, and bring it to the top of the work. Now insert the same finger through the first slit in the top strip, pick up the second strip from beneath, and bring it back to the top. Similarly insert the forefinger through the remaining slit in the top strip to pick up the final strip from below. Study fig. 42.2 carefully.

One end of the complete puzzle is turned back through the space between the two pieces of leaf, as indicated by the arrow in fig. 42.3.

Now straighten and rearrange the strips so that they look more attractive and interesting. This will take some experimenting. The final work should look like the puzzle in the photograph.

The game is to ask someone to undo the puzzle without splitting the flax. With a little practice the same puzzle can be made with more slits in the flax, making the problem appear more complex.

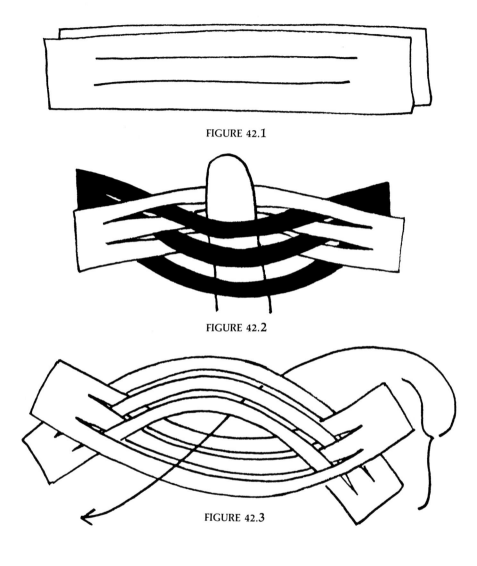

FIGURE 42.1

FIGURE 42.2

FIGURE 42.3

UNIT 43
Second puzzle

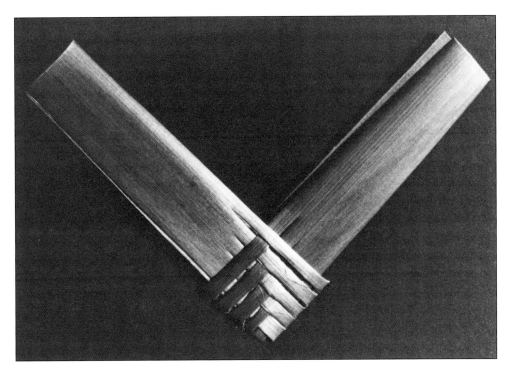

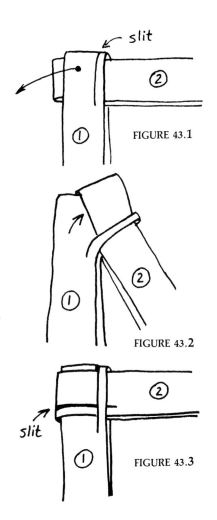

slit

FIGURE 43.1

FIGURE 43.2

slit

FIGURE 43.3

This second puzzle was shown to me by a boy from Malaita in the Solomon Islands in 1971.

Take two strips of leaf, fold each strip in half and insert strip 1 inside strip 2 as shown in fig. 43.1. Then make a slit in strip 1 as shown.

Remove the main section of strip 1 from strip 2 and insert it in strip 2, as shown in fig. 43.2, to lie in the position shown in fig. 43.3.

Now make a slit in strip 2 as shown in fig. 43.3. Remove the main section of strip 2 and insert it in the main section

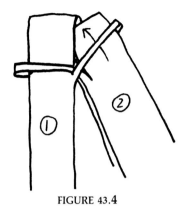

FIGURE 43.4

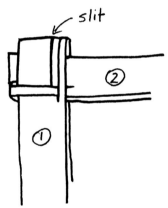

FIGURE 43.5

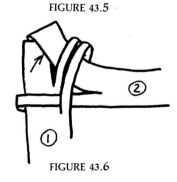

FIGURE 43.6

of strip 1, as shown in fig. 43.4, to lie in the position shown in fig. 43.5.

Make a second slit in strip 1, as shown in fig. 43.5. Remove the main section of strip 1 and insert it in the main section of strip 2, as in fig. 43.6, to lie in the position shown in fig. 43.7. Make a second slit in strip 2, as in fig. 43.7.

Remove the main section of strip 2 and insert it in the main section of strip 1, as in fig. 43.8.

Make another slit in strip 1. Remove the main section of strip 1 and insert it in the main section of strip 2. Continue in the same way until the full width of the strips has been used.

Again the game is to ask a person who has not seen how the puzzle is constructed to unravel it without splitting the strips.

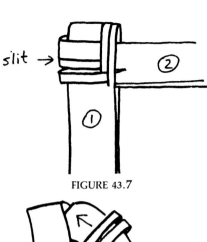

FIGURE 43.7

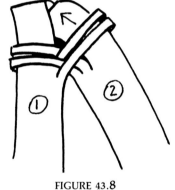

FIGURE 43.8

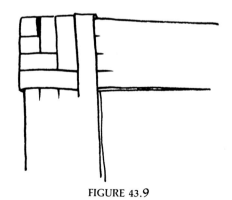

FIGURE 43.9

UNIT 44
Whistles

Coconut leaflet whistles are common in many islands in the Pacific, and Māori people in New Zealand made the same toy from the rito or flax shoot. The rito was pulled from the plant and then rolled into a cone. The flax whistle that survives today as a children's toy is a smaller version of makeshift bugles that were used to announce an approach to a village and were called tetere (Phillipps 1966).

Take a young central leaf from a flax plant. This is called the rito. Its removal is a knockback to the plant so it should not be removed from a young or valued plant. The rito can be removed from the plant by pulling on it.

The midrib of the rito is removed. Take one of the resulting halves of the leaf and wrap it around the index finger, starting at the pointed tip end. Remove the leaf from the finger and continue to roll it spirally into a cone shape as in fig. 44.1.

When it has all been rolled up the wide open end is secured with a narrow strip of flax which is tied around it. The whistle should look like fig. 44.2.

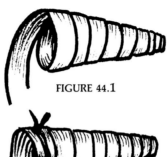

FIGURE 44.1

FIGURE 44.2

To blow, flatten the mouthpiece end together with the teeth, release it again and blow.

Longer bugles, called tetere, are also traditional, and can be made by adding new wider strips and continuing to wrap them onto the spiral cone as the old ones become used up (fig. 44.3). Using thicker leaves produces a whistle with a lower tone.

FIGURE 44.3

UNIT 45
Boat

This boat was taught to me by Hone Komene at Cape Runaway in 1965 but has a wide distribution with slight variations from district to district. In my experience these boats often capsize in the water. To stop them from tipping over, a pebble or small lump of clay is put in where it is needed to correct the balance. If the boat tends to sink, the secret then seems to be to make them quite large so that they displace a large surface area. Using lighter, drier flax from higher ground also helps.

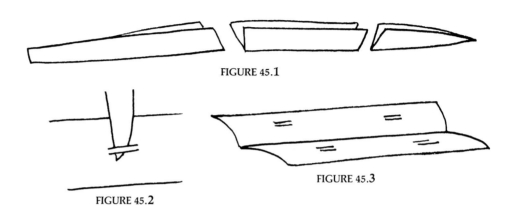

FIGURE 45.1

FIGURE 45.2

FIGURE 45.3

Take a single untreated leaf and cut out the middle section, as shown in fig. 45.1.

With a sharp pointed knife, cut slits in the leaf, as shown in fig. 45.2. The slits should not go right through the leaf but should penetrate only the upper surface. Lift the flax between the slits with the point of a knife, as in fig. 45.3.

Cut a small notch in the midrib at each end, as shown in fig. 45.4. Then cut the bow and stern to shape.

With a fingernail or a knife, make small slits in both ends of the boat, as shown in fig. 45.5.

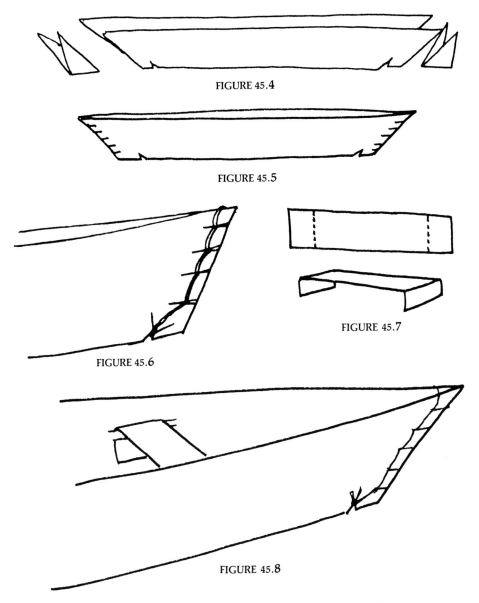

FIGURE 45.4

FIGURE 45.5

FIGURE 45.6

FIGURE 45.7

FIGURE 45.8

Thread a very fine thread of flax up through these slits, over the top of the boat, and then down the other side. Tie the two ends of the strip together in the notch (fig. 45.6). Repeat at the other end of the boat. The ends of the boat have now been sewn up.

The seats are made from strips of flax about 1 cm wide and as long as the width of the boat. The ends of each of these seats are folded down, as shown in fig. 45.7.

The ends of the seats are worked into the slits in the sides of the boat, as in fig. 45.8, and the boat is complete.

The flax will shrink and roll up as it dries so the boat will be attractive only on the day it is made, but children appear to find the most satisfaction in the actual construction.

If the boat is found to be top heavy when placed on the water, a small stone or some clay can be put in to balance it. If the boat sinks the flax that has been used is too heavy. Try to select a broad, soft, thin leaf and make the boat quite long — up to 60 cm.

To add a sail, cut a section about 25 cm long out of a leaf, as in fig. 45.9

Cut the section to shape, as in fig. 45.10, and fold along the dotted line A.

The protruding length of midrib, now folded, lies along the bottom of the hull under a seat. A fine thread of flax is attached to the bow, passes through a small slit in the top of the sail (marked B in fig. 45.10), and is tied to the stern, holding the sail in place.

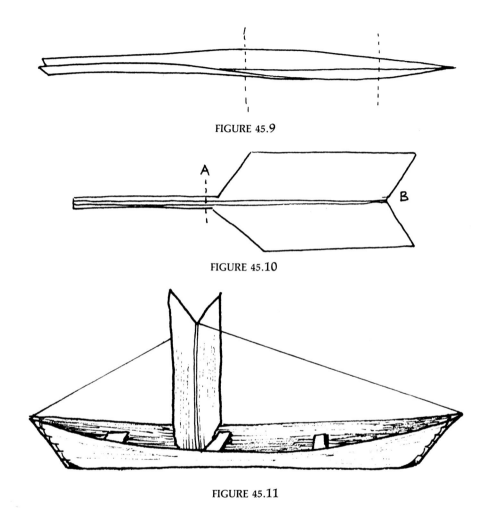

FIGURE 45.9

FIGURE 45.10

FIGURE 45.11

UNIT 46
Ngutu pārera (duck's bill)

This simple toy has amused many children and no doubt will amuse many more. A piece of the hard butt end of a flax leaf is split lengthwise, and one of these halves is folded back so that it becomes hinged. The toy is moved energetically up and down causing the flapping hinged section to clap against its partner, making a quacking noise. It is interesting to note that Pākeha children seeing the toy for the first time sometimes spontaneously remark, "Duck's bill!", which is the translation of the Māori term.

I first saw the toy when playing with George Kōti at Pōkeno as a child. He foretold that playing with it would bring rain, and on this occasion it did, much to the consternation of an unbeliever. The toy's association with rain-making seems to be as widely known as the toy itself.

The name ngutu pārera was given to me by Kohine Ponika of Tuhoe. Mrs Monica Isherwood of Tūwharetoa knew the same toy as pakipaki (to clap).

Cut off a butt end of flax about 30 cm long. Separate the two halves of the leaf for about a third of the length by forcing a knife between them. Fold the upper half of the split section back like a hinge. The toy is held by the other end and flapped sharply downwards so that the moving part smacks against the unhinged section, making a cracking sound.

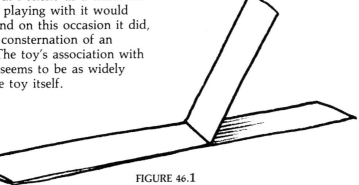

FIGURE 46.1

U N I T   4 7
Darts

The throwing of flax leaves as darts is an old game that has survived in some parts of New Zealand up to the present day. It was shown to me by Mossy Maangi and Taane Komene of Te Whānau ā Apanui at Cape Runaway in 1964. Kohine Ponika of Tuhoe calls the game pārere. I saw children at Kaitaia in 1976 using leaflets of nīkau in the same way, but they had no knowledge of the flax version.

Take a whole flax leaf and remove most of the hard butt end. From the butt end, partially tear away a narrow strip for about 20 cm along the keel of the leaf, as in fig. 47.1.

Hold the flax leaf on the right shoulder with the butt end forward. Take the narrow strip from the keel firmly in the right hand, and use the left hand to support the strip itself. A sudden jerk downward on the narrow strip will project the leaf forward with such force that the rest of the strip will be torn away from the main leaf.

A traditional sophistication shown to me by Mossy Maangi and Taane Komene at Cape Runaway is to attach the narrow strip to a throwing stick 30 to 60 cm long with a second narrow strip of flax. The leaf is either laid on the ground or placed against a log or something similar with the butt end pointing upwards and in the direction of the throw. With the stick held in the hand, the throw is made with a long, sweeping movement, reaching well back and then pulling the dart sharply forward past the body and flinging it as far in front as possible. This movement projects the dart at a much greater speed.

An updated version of the traditional dart is illustrated in fig. 47.3. It was invented by John Konui of Turangi in 1975 and is made in the same way, the front part of the jet being the hard butt part of the leaf and the wings being the two sides of the flax leaf. The strip torn away from the base and the throwing method are the same as for the dart described earlier.

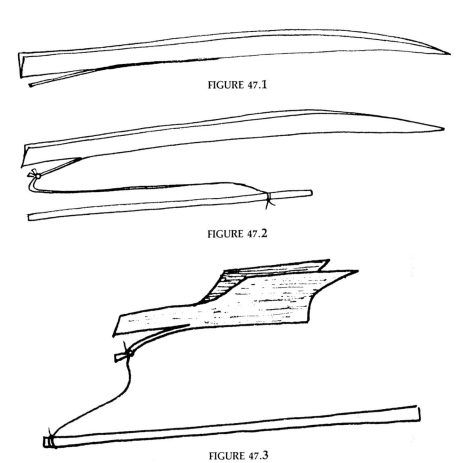

FIGURE 47.1

FIGURE 47.2

FIGURE 47.3

UNIT 48
Papakingaro (Māori fly swat)

The god's eye symbol appears in Asia, Australia, the Americas, Europe and the Pacific Islands but it is probably best known from Mexico, where it protects homes and brings good luck. In the Solomon Islands the same symbol is placed on house finials for protection

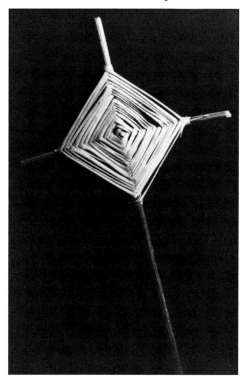

against evil. It is interesting to note that when it is placed at the tip of the ihiihi ornaments at the front of a war canoe it is called karu atua (god's eye) (Best 1925b). These symbols then become the eyes of the canoe and are endowed with great spiritual power. The fly fan or fly swat is also known as papaki rango, patu rango or patu ngaro.

Tie two sticks about 30 cm long into a cross. Prepare a number of strips of flax about 1 cm wide. Secure the butt end of one strip to the centre of the cross. Wrap the working strip once behind each of the sticks before passing on to the next stick. Allow the flax strips to overlap one another so that it is not possible to see between them.

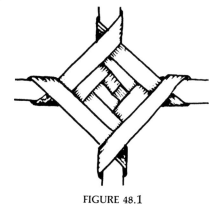

FIGURE 48.1

Fig. 48.1 shows the work from the front. Fig. 48.2 shows the work from behind.

When the working strip 1 in fig. 48.3 nears its end, insert a new strip 2 underneath it as shown.

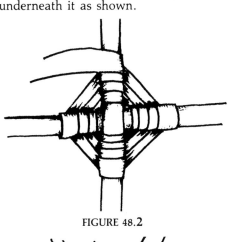

FIGURE 48.2

FIGURE 48.3

Strip 2 in fig. 48.3 is folded along the dotted line and carried in the direction indicated by the arrow. It is taken behind and around the stick before moving on to the next stick. If strip 2 is pulled firmly, it holds itself and the old strip 1 in place and no further tying is required.

More easily made, colourful versions can be made using coloured wool as is done in Mexico.

Sometimes two crossed sticks are used instead of one. The method of manufacture is the same but the result is a six-sided figure (fig. 48.4).

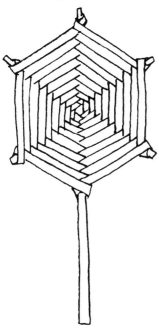

FIGURE 48.4

UNIT 49
Boat basket

A recent development, the boat basket has become popular in schools and with beginners, and is within the reach of ten years olds. I first saw it demonstrated by Mere Kururangi, specialist teacher in art and craft, when she gave lessons at Whangaparāoa School, Cape Runaway, about 1965 and have seen it often since.

I have also heard of a group of women who made them to hold flower arrangements for elderly patients in hospitals. It can be used as a substitute for a rourou or foodbasket when serving food from a hāngi or barbecue, or as a container for a decorative arrangement of fruit.

Prepare twelve strips of flax about 2 cm wide and 40 cm long. Plait them into a small mat as shown in fig. 49.1. There are five strips running one way and seven the other.

Fold strips 1 and 2 in fig. 49.1 back on themselves, as indicated by the arrows, to lie in the positions shown in fig. 49.2.

Fold strip 1 in fig. 49.2 along the dotted line, in the direction indicated by the arrow, to lie in the position shown in fig. 49.3.

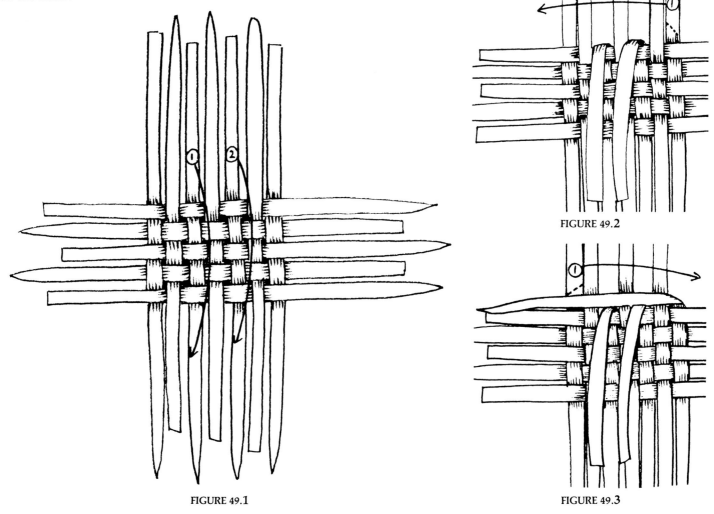

FIGURE 49.1

FIGURE 49.2

FIGURE 49.3

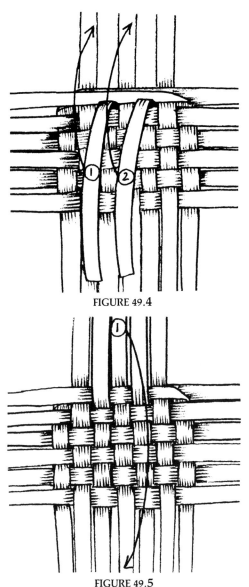

FIGURE 49.4

Fold strip 1 in fig. 49.3 along the dotted line, in the direction indicated by the arrow, to lie in the position shown in fig. 49.4. It will need to be placed beneath the previous strip.

Return strips 1 and 2 in fig. 49.4 to their original positions, as indicated by the arrows. The work will now look like fig. 49.5.

Fold strip 1 in fig. 49.5 back on itself, as indicated by the arrow, to lie in the position shown in fig. 49.6

Fold strip 1 in fig. 49.6 along the dotted line and in the direction indicated by the arrow.

Fold strip 2 in fig. 49.6 along the dotted line and in the direction indicated by the arrow. One strip will have to lie on top of the other, as shown in fig. 49.7.

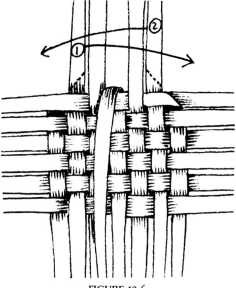

FIGURE 49.6

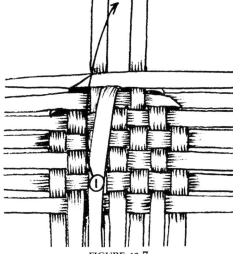

FIGURE 49.7

FIGURE 49.5

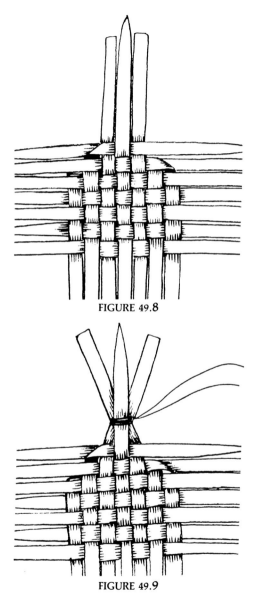

FIGURE 49.8

FIGURE 49.9

Return strip 1 in fig. 49.7 to its original position, as indicated by the arrow and shown in fig. 49.8.

Tie the three remaining strips together with a thin strip of flax, as shown in fig. 49.9. Tie as close as possible to the main body of the work. Do not cut off the ends of the tie as these are used later.

Turn the work around and work the opposite side in the same way following figs. 49.1 to 49.9. The work will now look like fig. 49.10.

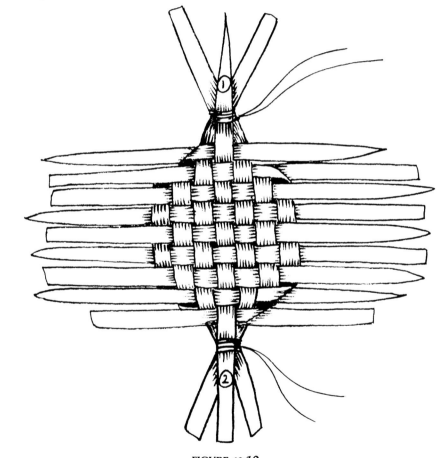

FIGURE 49.10

Bring the central strip 1 in fig. 49.10 over in a curve and introduce it to the work on the other side of the basket and at the opposite end of the same strip (marked 2). In the same way strip 2 is brought over and into the main body of the work at point 1. See fig. 49.11. The two ends of the same strip form the arch that is to become the handle.

Strips 1 and 2 in fig. 49.11 are now wrapped around the handle as in fig. 49.12.

When the strips reach the other side of the basket, they are tied in place with the narrow strip of flax left there earlier. Strips 3 and 4 in fig. 49.11 are now wrapped around the handle in the same manner and tied on the opposite side.

FIGURE 49.12

The strips bracketed together and labelled 5 in fig. 49.11 are now bundled together to form one end of the basket. The neatest way to do this is to take the central strip and then add a strip alternately from either side on top of it. Then add the next pair in the same way, and so on. When all the strips from one end are neatly arranged together, tie them tightly with a narrow strip of flax.

At this stage the basket is gently shaped away from its flat mat shape and into a hollow boat shape. The strips at the other end are then gathered together and tied. Trim off the ends to shape and the basket is complete.

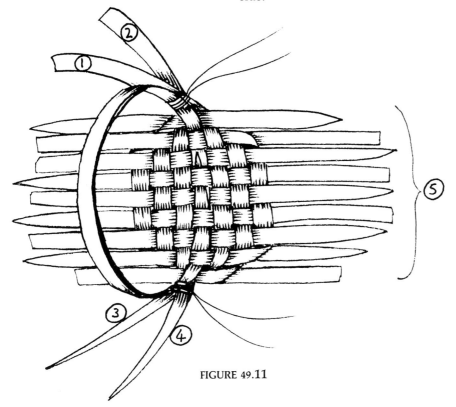

FIGURE 49.11

UNIT 50
Rourou (food baskets)

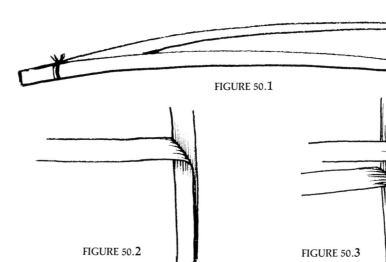

FIGURE 50.1

FIGURE 50.2

FIGURE 50.3

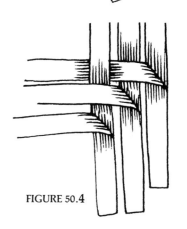

FIGURE 50.4

These are the food platters made from green flax which took the place of plates and dishes for the old time Māori and are still sometimes seen at hui where food is consumed. There are numerous names for such a small article. Among them are pārō, konae, kono, kōpae, pohewa, tipoti and there are many others. In the Pacific Islands the leaves on which food is served are called raurau.

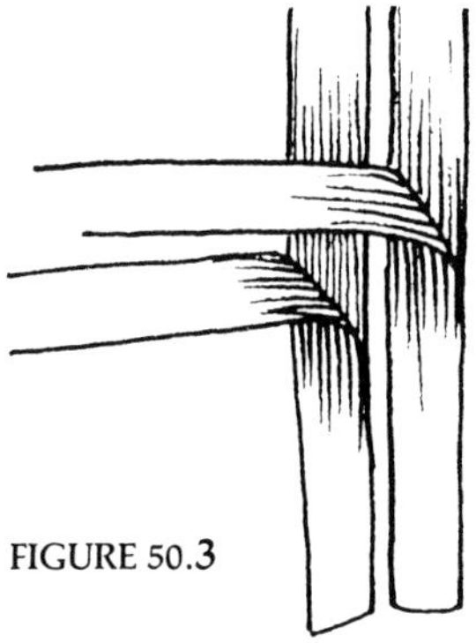

Take four flax leaves and remove the outer edges and the midribs of each, leaving them joined for about 8 cm at the butt ends. If they split apart they can be tied together as in fig. 50.1. The leaves are not normally scraped or softened but may be if preferred.

Take the first pair of strips and lay them on the floor, as in fig 50.2.

Lay a second pair to the right of the first pair, as in fig. 50.3

A third pair is added on the right and plaited in, as in fig. 50.4.

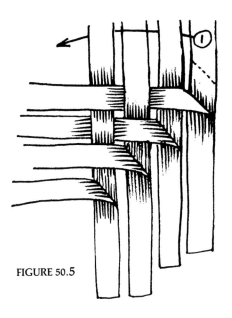

FIGURE 50.5

The final pair of strips is added on the right and plaited in, as in fig. 50.5.

Fold strip 1 in fig. 50.5 along the dotted line and plait it, as indicated by the arrow, to lie in the position shown in fig. 50.6. The surface of the leaf is changed.

In the same way, strip 1 in fig. 50.6 is folded along the dotted line and plaited in the direction indicated by the arrow to lie in the position shown in fig. 50.7.

Strip 1 in fig. 50.7 is folded along the dotted line and plaited in the direction indicated to lie in the position shown in fig. 50.8. There is now only one strip protruding above.

The work is now picked up and held on the lap. Turn the work around so that the single protruding strip is to the right, as in fig. 50.8.

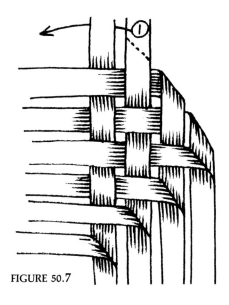

FIGURE 50.7

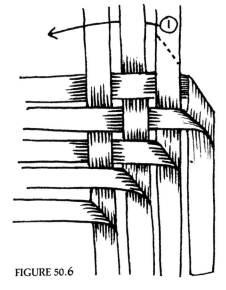

FIGURE 50.6

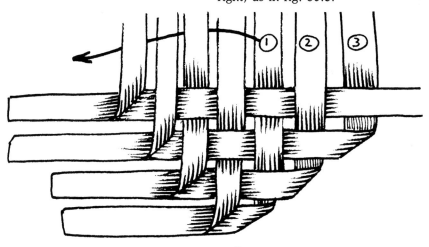

FIGURE 50.8

Leave strips 2 and 3 as they are and move strip 1 as indicated. During this movement the first corner is formed at the point marked * in fig. 50.9. The surface of strip 1 is not changed; that is, the same surface remains uppermost. Fig. 50.9 shows the work in a flat, diagrammatic form.

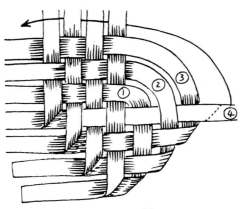

FIGURE 50.11

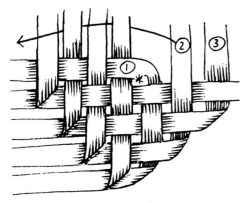

FIGURE 50.9

Strip 4 in fig. 50.11 is *folded* along the dotted line and moved as indicated by the arrow to the position shown in fig. 50.13.

Strip 1 in fig. 50.13 is folded along the dotted line and moved in the direction indicated to lie in the position shown in fig. 50.14.

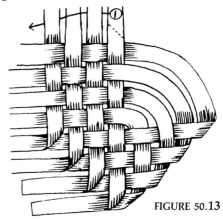

FIGURE 50.13

FIGURE 50.12

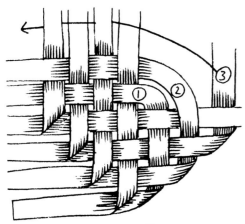

FIGURE 50.10

Strip 2 in fig. 50.9 is plaited in the direction indicated to lie in the position shown in fig. 50.10.

Strip 3 in fig. 50.10 is plaited in the direction indicated by the arrow to the position shown in fig. 50.11. The surface of the leaf is not changed. The work should now look like fig. 50.12.

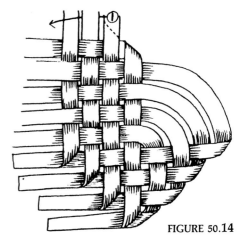

FIGURE 50.14

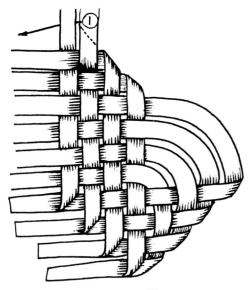

FIGURE 50.15

Continue to work following the directions from fig. 50.9 until only one strip projects from the side and the second corner is formed. Four corners are made in this way, but for the last one the strips are plaited back into the base of the basket. Beginning with the centre strip, each strip is plaited along the top of the strip in the base that matches it. They are plaited under a couple of strips until the work is secure and the waste ends are then cut off.

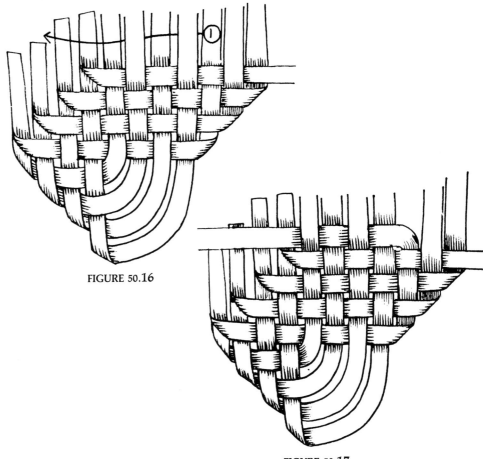

FIGURE 50.16

Fold strip 1 in fig. 50.14 along the dotted line and in the direction indicated to the position shown in fig. 50.15.

Fold strip 1 in fig. 50.15 along the dotted line and move as indicated by the arrow. There is now a single strip left protruding as there was in fig. 50.8.

Turn the work around so that the single strip protrudes to the right. Strip 1 in fig. 50.16 is plaited in the direction indicated by the arrow to the position shown in fig. 50.17. The strip is *not* folded and the same surface remains uppermost. The movement is the same as that in figs. 50.8 and 50.9.

FIGURE 50.17